Spellography

A Student Road Map to Better Spelling

Teacher Answer Guide

Book B

Louisa Moats, Ed.D.
and
Bruce Rosow, M.A.

ISBN 1-57035-608-4

Edited by Karen Butler and Sandra L. Knauke
Text layout and design by Sue Campbell and Sherri Rowe
Cover design by Sue Campbell
Production assistance by Eileen Bechtold and Tracy Katzenberger
Illustrated by Tom Zilis

13 12 11 10 RRDMIDWI 6 5 4 3 2

Printed in the United States of America
Published and Distributed by

SOPRIS
WEST

4093 Specialty Place • Longmont, Colorado 80504
(303) 651-2829 • www. sopriswest.com

Contents

Lessons 11-20 are preceded by two pages of Phonemic Awareness Activities for the teacher to use in class. These pages appear only in the Teacher Answer Guide.

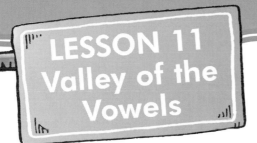

1. **Identify the Vowel Sound** Identify the vowel sound in each of these words. Say that vowel sound alone. Then, find the sound on the Vowel Sounds Chart.

Set A: /ā/, /ă/, /ē/, /ĕ/, /ī/, /ĭ/, /ō/, /ŏ/, /ū/, /ŭ/

bead /ē/	bed /ĕ/	bad /ă/	booed /ū/	bud /ŭ/
note /ō/	not /ŏ/	neat /ē/	net /ĕ/	knit /ĭ/
tub /ŭ/	tube /ū/	peak /ē/	pick /ĭ/	peck /ĕ/
bite /ī/	bit /ĭ/	bet /ĕ/	boat /ō/	boot /ū/
mitt /ĭ/	met /ĕ/	moat /ō/	moot /ū/	mutt /ŭ/
grace /ā/	grass /ă/	slept /ĕ/	slipped /ĭ/	sloped /ō/

Set B: /aw/, /ŏ/, /ŭ/

Don /ŏ/	dawn /aw/	done /ŭ/	paw /aw/	pat /ă/
caught /aw/	cot /ŏ/	cut /ŭ/	pot /ŏ/	putt /ŭ/
bald /aw/	bulk /ŭ/	odd /ŏ/	awed /aw/	flood /ŭ/

Set C: /ū/, /ŭ/, /ō/, /o͝o/

noon /ū/	known /ō/	none /ŭ/	put /o͝o/	putt /ŭ/
cope /ō/	cup /ŭ/	loop /ū/	huff /ŭ/	hoof /o͝o/
mud /ŭ/	mowed /ō/	mood /ū/	stood /o͝o/	stud /ŭ/
shuck /ŭ/	shook /o͝o/	Huck /ŭ/	hook /o͝o/	oak /ō/

Phonemic Awareness Activities (Continued)

2. **Substitution Task** Substitute the first sound with the second sound to make a new word.

kite /ī/ – /ĭ/	mute /yū/ – /ŭ/	hope /ō/ – /ŏ/	mate /ā/ – /ă/
pile /ī/ – /ĭ/	plume /ū/ – /ŭ/	Pete /ē/ – /ĕ/	lake /ā/ – /ă/
gate /ā/ – /ĕ/	fine /ī/ – /ĭ/	grape /ā/ – /ĭ/	quote /ō/ – /ĭ/
tube /ū/ – /ă/	grain /ā/ – /ĭ/	vine /ī/ – /ă/	lute /ū/ – /ĕ/
make /ā/ – /ŭ/	fuse /yū/ – /ŭ/	fine /ī/ – /ă/	cone /ō/ – /ă/
stole /ō/ – /ĭ/	mute /yū/ – /ĭ/	coat /ō/ – /ŏ/	gait /ā/ – /ŭ/

3. **Sound Reversals** Reverse the sounds (phonemes) to make a new word (**pit** – **tip**).

late – tail	mace – same	aid – day	feel – leaf
zone – nose	no – own	say – ace	sigh – ice
dude – dude	right – tire	nail – lane	foe – oaf
day – aid	scale – lakes	Nile – line	stow – oats

LESSON 11
Valley of the Vowels

Make copies of the Concept Quiz so that students can take it again at the end of this lesson to see what they've learned.

Concept Quiz

Name _____ Date _____

1. How many speech sounds (**phonemes**) are there in English? _40+_

2. How many vowel letters are there in English? _Six_ (a, e, i, o, u, and y)

3. In what ways could the inventors of English spelling have done a better job?

   See * for example answers. _____

   _____

4. What's the difference between vowel sounds and consonant sounds?

   Vowel sounds are **open** sounds, made without blocking the vocal airstream.

   Consonant sounds are **blocked**, or obstructed, sounds made as the vocal

   airstream is blocked by our lips, teeth, tongue, or nose.

5. **True or False:** Every syllable in English has a vowel sound. _T**_

6. Give an example word for each of the spellings you know for these sounds. Underline the letters in each word that represent that sound.

/ā/ (as in **ape**)	/ē/ (as in **east**)	/ī/ (as in **ice**)	/ō/ (as in **open**)	/ū/ (as in **moo**)
See *** for example responses.				

7. Underline the word in each group that has a different vowel sound.

   a. third, word, <u>merit</u>, splurge

   b. hoof, <u>proof</u>, stood, shook

   c. ball, claw, <u>bowl</u>, halt

   d. boost, stew, <u>throne</u>, mood

   e. peak, reed, <u>bread</u>, deal

   f. plow, <u>blow</u>, now, cow

Lesson 11 • *Valley of the Vowels*   1

8. Give two examples of **diphthongs**—vowel sounds that slide in the middle and sound as if they have two parts.
   Examples answers:

   /ou/ (cow, out)   /oi/ (boy, oil)

9. For each of these words, indicate with a circle whether the vowel sound is made with the mouth in a smiley shape or a puckered, rounded shape.

meet	**note**	**ape**
(smiley)/ round	smiley /(round)	(smiley)/ round
saw	**it**	**boot**
smiley /(round)	(smiley)/ round	smiley /(round)

10. How many different types of syllables are there? _Six_
    Give an example word for each syllable type.

    See **** for example responses.
    _____

    _____

*   (1) Words could be spelled just the way they sound (**little/lidl**). (2) Each letter could represent just one sound. (3) All the letter sounds could be represented by a different single letter (like the phonetic alphabet). (4) No silent letters. (5) No irregular past tense (**go/went /gone, sing/ sang/sung**) or plural words (**goose/geese**). (6) Always have a doubled consonant after an initial short vowel (**ever/evver, radish/raddish**) so that spellings can't be confused with single consonants after an initial long vowel (as in **even** or **radar**). (7) Use a picture language.

**   This statement is mostly true, but there are some mucky examples that murk things up. There are words like **rhy–thm**, for example, that don't have a vowel letter in the second syllable; words like **lit–tle** and **muz–zle** don't have much of a vowel sound in the final syllable. The main ideas, however, are that virtually every syllable in the English language is built around a vowel sound, and the number of sounded vowels in a word is equal to the number of syllables in that word.

***   Students should not be expected to come up with all of the different spellings for these long vowel sounds at this point. The idea is to determine what they know initially and what they learn in this lesson about long-vowel spellings. Some possible responses include:

/ā/	baby, rain, play, steak, vein, eight, they	/ō/	pony, rope, boat, glow, doe
/ē/	even, eat, see, piece, these, happy, monkey, receive	/ū/	food, rumor, soup, dude, grew, true
/ī/	item, smile, dry, high, type, pie		

**** Students will be introduced to syllable types in this lesson, so definitions of the different types are not expected. Again, the idea is to compare what students initially know to what they will learn—in this case—about syllable types. The next several lessons will circle back and look at each syllable type.

Closed (single short vowel followed by one or more consonant guards): m**e**t, s**i**t, **a**t, b**a**th, d**o**dge, m**u**d, **i**tch

Open (syllable ends with a single, unguarded vowel that usually gives its long sound): b**a**–by, m**e**–ter, **i**–tem, **o**–pen, m**u**–sic, t**i**–ny

vc + -e (a single vowel followed by a single consonant + a silent **e**, which signals that the vowel sound is long): s**i**te, m**a**de, **e**ve, r**o**pe, m**u**le

Vowel Team (two vowel letters that represent one vowel sound): t**ea**m, b**oa**t, p**ie**, b**ai**t, bl**ue**

v + -r (a vowel—or sometimes a vowel team—followed by an **r** in the same syllable): b**ir**d, t**ar**, **ear**, f**ur**, **ear**–ly, c**or**n

c + -le (a consonant followed by the letters **le** in the final syllable, giving the syllable a muted schwa + /l/ sound): cy–c**le**, ma–p**le**, ea–g**le**, ruf–f**le**, tur–t**le**

Vowel Sounds Chart

(By order of articulation, with spelling examples)

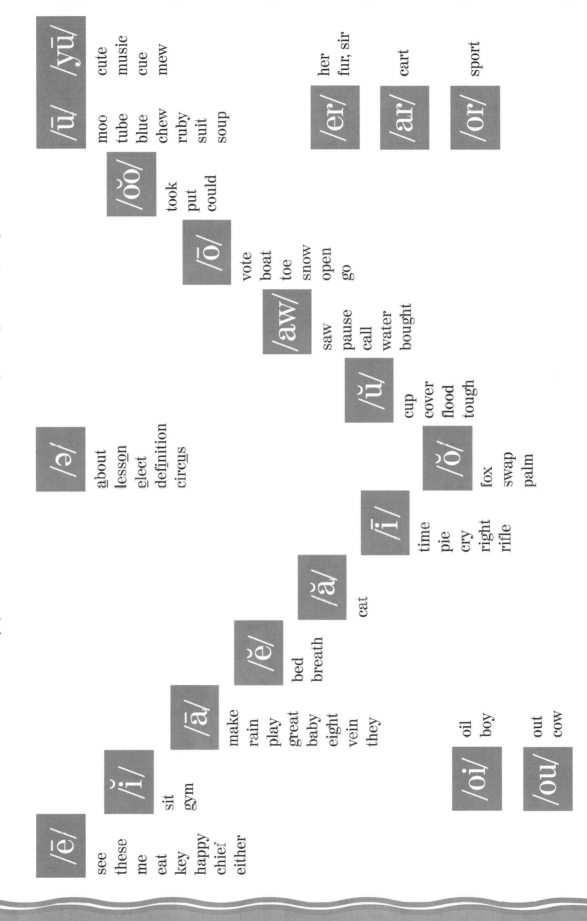

/ē/
see
these
me
eat
key
happy
chief
either

/ĭ/
sit
gym

/ā/
make
rain
play
great
baby
eight
vein
they

/ĕ/
bed
breath

/ă/
cat

/e/
about
lesson
elect
definition
circus

/ū/ /yū/
cute
music
cue
mew
moo
tube
blue
chew
ruby
suit
soup

/oͦo/
took
put
could

/ō/
vote
boat
toe
snow
open
go

/aw/
saw
pause
call
water
bought

/ŭ/
cup
cover
flood
tough

/ī/
time
pie
cry
right
rifle

/ŏ/
fox
swap
palm

/er/
her
fur, sir

/ar/
cart

/or/
sport

/oi/
oil
boy

/ou/
out
cow

Exercise 1

Vowel Identification Listen while your teacher says three words in each group. Say the two words in each group that have the same vowel sound.

Students should respond with the underlined words.

<u>call</u>, fork, <u>bought</u>	<u>fort</u>, slaw, <u>poor</u>	<u>press</u>, <u>bread</u>, stitch	<u>must</u>, <u>flood</u>, boot
<u>drown</u>, fault, <u>crowd</u>	store, <u>park</u>, <u>arm</u>	flute, <u>stoke</u>, <u>mow</u>	<u>starry</u>, <u>merry</u>, <u>cherry</u>
<u>joist</u>, jaw, <u>joy</u>	<u>time</u>, catch, <u>pie</u>	fist, <u>fenced</u>, <u>rest</u>	<u>fill</u>, gel, <u>stiff</u>

Did you disagree with anyone? It's likely, because the dialect of English you speak may be different from the dialect of someone who comes from another part of the United States.

Spelling Concept: There are 18 vowel sounds in English, including the three vowel + **-r** (**v + -r**) sounds and two diphthong vowel sounds in our Vowel Sounds Chart. These vowel sounds are distinguished by the way the mouth is shaped and the tongue is held. All vowels are open, continuous, voiced sounds.

A vowel is *not* a consonant! Vowels are like cats, and consonants are like dogs. Just as cats think that they are superior to dogs, vowels think that they are better than consonants. Vowels believe they are more expressive and more interesting than consonants. Consonants think vowels are flighty and unreliable and that vowels need consonants to keep them in line. Even though vowels are cats and consonants are dogs, both find ways to get along and work together for the sake of the English language. In truth, each would be bored without the other.

Consonants are *closed* speech sounds. The lips, teeth, and/or tongue obstruct the airflow when consonants are formed. Many consonant sounds just close down and stop after they are made. Consonants also close in and guard vowels in closed syllables.

Vowels are *open* speech sounds. The airflow is unobstructed. Because they are open-ended, vowel sounds can be held and carried, or sung.

Music Time! Sing the first line of the United States' national anthem. Then, in the space below each word, give the symbol for each vowel sound, using the Vowel Sounds Chart as a source of symbols. Finally, sing this line again, crooning only the vowel sounds.

Oh	say	can	you	see	by	the	dawn's	early	light
/ō/	/ā/	/ă/	/ū/	/ē/	/ī/	/ŭ/	/aw/	/er/	/ē/ /ī/

Syllables are units of speech formed around a vowel sound. Every syllable has a vowel sound. There are many syllables built with just one vowel (**o**–bey, **e**–ven), but there are no syllables built with just one consonant. Only a few oddball syllables have a vowel sound but no vowel letter (like rhy–**thm**).

Spelling Concept: English vowel spellings are challenging. The first writers had only six vowel letters—**a**, **e**, **i**, **o**, **u**, and **y**—to spell 18 vowel sounds. That means that those letters are often doubled up. It takes lots of teamwork among vowel letters to spell all of the vowel sounds.

Exercise 3

Underline the letters and letter combinations that spell all the vowel sounds in this sentence. Then, answer the questions that follow the sentence.

Th<u>e</u> gr<u>ay</u>-h<u>ai</u>red th<u>ie</u>f—<u>a</u>rmed w<u>i</u>th <u>a</u> kn<u>ife</u> <u>a</u>nd h<u>a</u>ndg<u>u</u>n— p<u>au</u>sed <u>o</u>n th<u>e</u> r<u>oo</u>ft<u>o</u>p, wh<u>i</u>ch w<u>a</u>s c<u>o</u>v<u>e</u>red w<u>i</u>th s<u>oo</u>t fr<u>o</u>m <u>eigh</u>t sm<u>o</u>k<u>y</u> ch<u>i</u>mn<u>ey</u>s.

1. How many syllables did you find? _28_

2. Is the number of syllables the same as the number of vowel letters? _No_

3. Is the number of syllables you found the same as the number of vowel sounds you heard? _Yes_

4. How many vowel sounds were spelled with teams of vowel letters?
   Nine, if you count vc + -e spellings (knife) and air from haired. If you
   include the v + -r spellings (armed, covered), then there are 11.

5. Find an example of the same vowel sound being spelled different ways.
   /ā/ (gray, eight)   /ē/ (thief, smoky, chimneys)

6. Find a vowel sound that is spelled with four letters working together.
   /ā/ (eight)

Spelling Concept: The 18 vowel sounds in the Vowel Sounds Chart can be arranged in a way that shows how they are pronounced. Some are made in the front of the mouth, others in the back. At the beginning of this lesson, the Vowel Sounds Chart arranges the sounds in the shape of a valley to show how the jaw changes position for each new vowel.

The mouth begins with a smile and the jaw fairly closed. After the /ē/ (as in **see**), each step to a new vowel is taken by dropping the jaw a little bit until the vowel /ŏ/ (as in **ox**) is reached. That's the lowest, open vowel—so naturally, when a doctor wants to look in your throat, he or she wants you to say /ŏ/ ("ahh"). Vowel sounds are made from there by pulling back the tongue, rounding the lips, and closing the jaw step by step, until we get to /ū/ (as in **tube**). **Schwa**—/ə/—the dreaded, unaccented, and indistinct vowel, floats in the middle of the mouth. The **diphthongs** /oi/ and /ou/ are sliders. Watch your lips slide out to the side or into the middle as you say /oi/ (**boy**) and /ou/ (**cow**). The vowel + **-r** (**v + -r**) patterns show that vowels followed by the /r/ sound are changed by the influence of /r/.

Spelling Concept: There are four groups of vowels—long, short, diphthong, and vowel + **-r** (**v + -r**) vowels. The diphthongs are /oi/ (as in **boy**) and /ou/ (as in **out**); they slide in the middle. The vowel sound /ŏŏ/ (as in **book**) and the vowel sound /aw/ (as in **saw**) belong with the short vowels for pronunciation, but have more varied spellings than the ones you have used in closed syllables.

Vowel Sounds Chart
(By order of articulation, with spelling examples)

Exercise 4

Fill in the blank Vowel Sounds Chart (at left) as you answer these questions. If necessary, you may refer to the master Vowel Sounds Chart at the beginning of this lesson.

a. List in order the seven short and long vowel sounds on the left side of the chart, working from top-left toward the bottom-center. Say them in order until you have mastered their pronunciations.

/ē/ (see) /ĭ/ (sit) /ā/ (make) /ĕ/ (bed) /ă/ (apple) /ī/ (time) /ŏ/ (fox)

b. Which vowel sounds on the left side of the chart are the most difficult to distinguish from each other? Why?

The sounds /ĭ/ and /ĕ/ and the sounds /ă/ and /ŏ/ are sometimes

difficult for students to distinguish. Both pairs are near each other

on the Vowel Sounds Chart because their sounds are produced in

the same part of the mouth, in a similar position. They feel and

sound similar.

c. Fill in the last four short and long vowel sounds on the right side of the chart, starting with /aw/ and working your way up to the upper right corner. These sounds are made with the mouth in a rounded position (like a /w/). Practice the pronunciations until you can say them in order, going toward the upper right corner.

/aw/ (saw) /ō/ (vote) /ŏŏ/ (took) /ū/ (moo)

d. The sound /ŭ/ (as in **cup**) is the **accented** form of the sound of schwa (/ə/). (You will be learning about the unaccented form, too.) Add both the /ŭ/ sound symbol and the schwa symbol /ə/ to your chart.

e. You have been working with closed syllables that have short vowel sounds. On the chart, locate and circle the five familiar short vowel sounds, along with /aw/ (as in **saw**) and /ŏŏ/ (as in **took**). Practice saying these sounds in order, from left to right.

/ĭ/ (itch) /ĕ/ (Ed) /ă/ (apple) /ŏ/ (odd) /ŭ/ (up) /aw/ (saw) /ŏŏ/ (book)

f. You will be learning the spellings for the long vowel sounds. Put a star above each of these long vowel sounds on your chart and say them in order, from left to right.

/ē/ (me) /ā/ (ape) /ī/ (ice) /ō/ (oat) /ū/ (moo) /yū/ (you)

Exercise 5

Decked Out Make a card for each vowel sound. Put the sound symbol on one side and the spellings for the sound on the other. Arrange these vowel cards in the same order and pattern that they are on the Vowel Sounds Chart. Use these cards to work on memorizing the Valley of the Vowels. Then, answer these questions.

a. Which two vowel sounds have the greatest number of possible spellings?

___/ē/___   ___/ā/___

b. Which vowel sound is a high, front, smiley, long vowel sound?

___/ē/___

c. Make up a riddle about one of the vowel sounds and ask a classmate to solve your riddle.

_____

_____

_____

Example answers:

I'm the low-down sound the doctor makes you say. /ŏ/ (**hot**)

When you add this round sound to <u>ful</u>, you're terrible. /aw/ (**awful**)

I'm the short-vowel middle sound of a primary color. /ĕ/ (**red**)

Say this highest, smiley sound while I take your picture. /ē/ (**cheese**)

Not Out of Sorts Sort these three sets of words, which have been split into smiley, open, and round vowel sound groups. If you prefer, work with a group.

All words with a star (★) are example answers for Exercise #6b.

Set 1: babe   pat   pie   be   pet   pit   flea   beg   fly   bag   big   paid

/ē/ (as in **pea**)	/ĭ/ (as in **bit**)	/ā/ (as in **ape**)	/ĕ/ (as in **bet**)	/ă/ (as in **bat**)	/ī/ (as in **ice**)
flea	pit	babe	beg	pat	pie
be	big	paid	pet	bag	fly
see ★	tip ★	day ★	leg ★	ram ★	mice ★
be ★	chip ★	date ★	keg ★	cram ★	ice ★

Set 2:

blood   caught   swat   pod   fought
love   father   off   mom   putt
thought   trouble   laundry   of

Set 3:

hood   food   go   soup   stow
push   joke   cook   loaf
kook   stood   stewed

/aw/ (as in **saw**)	/ŏ/ (as in **ox**)	/ŭ/ (as in **up**)	/ō/ (as in **oat**)	/oo/ (aš in **book**)	/ū/ (as in **boot**)
caught	mom	blood	joke	hood	food
off	pod	putt	go	cook	kook
thought	father	trouble	loaf	stood	stewed
laundry	swat	love	stow	push	soup
fought	cod ★	of	snow ★	could ★	noodle ★
awful ★	rod ★	mutt ★	coat ★	hook ★	dune ★
auto ★	shot ★	rush ★	note ★	put ★	school ★

Exercise 6b

Now, go back to Exercise #6a and add two new words for each vowel sound. Put a star (★) next to the words you add.

Exercise 7

Make a recording of the Vowel Sounds Chart, with vowels spoken in order from top-left to top-right. First, say the vowel sounds as you look at the chart. Then, try to say the sounds from memory. (Some people remember them more easily by pairing a gesture or a key word with each sound.)

Spelling Concept: Each syllable type is for spelling a specific kind of vowel.

We will learn five more syllable types in addition to the closed syllables with short vowel sounds you have learned in Lessons 1–10.

1. **Open** syllable (long vowel sound with one letter): **ta**–ble, **ro**–bot, **e**–ven, **u**–ni–corn, **i**–con

2. **vowel + consonant + silent -e (vc + -e)** syllable (long vowel sound): h**ope**, m**ake**, P**ete**, t**ube**, **ice**

3. **Vowel Team** syllable (long vowel sound, short vowel sound, or diphthong): r**ai**n, **ou**t, **oi**l, ch**ie**f, b**oa**t, h**ea**d

4. **consonant + -le (c + -le)** syllable (final syllable, unaccented): a–**ble**, hag–**gle**, noz–**zle**, lit–**tle**

5. **vowel + -r (v + -r)** syllable (special vowel sounds with /r/): **ar**, **or**, **er**, **ur**, **ir**

Exercise 8

Sort these words based on their syllable type. Star (★) the words with two syllables that fit in two different groups.

cab	ace	wait	jerk	table	baby	me	path
pipe	sea	idle	firm	sit	rope	go	boat
gurgle	crush	oil	tart	unit	cute	ripple	chief

Closed Syllable
(as in **cob, set, must**)

cab

sit

crush

path

rip-ple ★

u-nit ★

Open Syllable
(as in **she, by, hobo**)

me

go

i-dle ★

u-nit ★

ta-ble ★

ba-by ★

vc + -e Syllable
(as in **cake, home, type**)

pipe

cute

rope

ace

v + -r Syllable
(as in **sir, fur, bar, born**)

jerk

firm

tart

gur-gle ★

c + -le Syllable
(as in **cycle, pickle**)

gur-gle ★

rip-ple ★

ta-ble ★

i-dle ★

Vowel Team Syllable
(as in **eat, day, bait, oat, see**)

sea

oil

chief

wait

boat

Spelling Concept: Schwa Blah! We have saved the worst—the evil and sinister **schwa**—for last.

The schwa is like a vampire; it sucks the sound out of vowels in unaccented syllables, leaving them muffled and lifeless. Schwa vowels are often misspelled because any vowel can be reduced to schwa (symbol: /ə/). For poor spellers, schwa vowels are the black holes of the universe. However, don't despair; learning about schwa vowels can help!

To learn about the schwa, you must first learn about accent. When words are two or more syllables long, some syllables can be **unaccented**. The following **bold** word has the same spelling in both sentences, but its meaning (and part of speech) changes when the accent shifts from the second syllable to the first syllable:

I **object** to this nonsense!

The **object** looked and felt like a worm.

 **Exercise 9**

Pick one of these word pairs. Use the words in two sentences that demonstrate how the meaning—and part of speech—changes when the syllable accent (indicated in **bold**) shifts.

record–re**cord**   **con**duct–con**duct**   **con**vict–con**vict**

1. _____

    _____

2. _____

    _____

Example answers:

record–re**cord**
1. The new **re**cord for loudest snoring goes to Uncle Fred. (noun)
2. We will re**cord** Uncle Fred one afternoon when he's going like a buzz saw. (verb)

conduct–con**duct**
1. "Your **con**duct is despicable, as usual," moaned Mom. (noun)
2. Bernstein wanted to con**duct** Thunker's Third Symphony. (verb)

convict–con**vict**
1. The **con**vict escaped for the third time. (noun)
2. The lawyers should be able to con**vict** him with this evidence. (verb)

 **Exercise 10**

Schwa Wah Read these **bold** single syllables and their example word pairs from left to right. Notice how the vowel sound of the single syllable is pronounced differently when used as an *unaccented syllable* in the two words that follow. These syllables have been placed under the dreaded influence of the schwa. *Ugh!*

cal	local	vocal	**pet**	carpet	trumpet
ton	cotton	button	**ten**	rotten	molten
pen	open	aspen	**ven**	even	Steven
age	image	village	**dom**	wisdom	kingdom
tain	captain	certain	**mon**	summon	salmon

Congratulations! You have just completed a tour of the Valley of the Vowels and the syllables they live in. We know it's not like taking a tour of Jupiter or Aruba, but we hope you liked it. Now, go back to the beginning and take the Concept Quiz again.

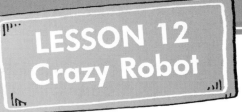

Phonemic Awareness Activities

1. **Identify the Vowel Sound** Listen for and identify the vowel sound in the **first** syllable of each of these words. Say that vowel sound alone. Then, find the sound on the Vowel Sounds Chart.

cable /ā/	**cabin** /ă/	**lilac** /ī/	**limit** /ĭ/	**even** /ē/
copilot /ō/	**ever** /ĕ/	**puny** /yū/	**punish** /ŭ/	
static /ă/	**secret** /ē/	**visit** /ĭ/	**station** /ā/	**proper** /ŏ/
visor /ī/	**human** /yū/	**second** /ĕ/	**propel** /ō/	**humming** /ŭ/
vanish /ă/	**finish** /ĭ/	**ruby** /ū/	**legal** /ē/	**closet** /ŏ/
level /ĕ/	**closer** /ō/	**vacant** /ā/	**final** /ī/	**rubbing** /ŭ/

2. **Segmentation Activity** Hold up the number of fingers—or show the number of markers—that is equal to the number of sounds (phonemes) in each of these words.

Oh	**so**	**solo**	**ray**	**craze**	**crazy**
/ō/	/s/ /ō/	/s/ /ō/ /l/ /ō/	/r/ /ā/	/k/ /r/ /ā/ /z/	/k/ /r/ /ā/ /z/ /ē/

knee	**tie**	**tiny**	**whip**	**equip**
/n/ /ē/	/t/ /ī/	/t/ /ī/ /n/ /ē/	/wh/ /ĭ/ /p/	/ē/ /k/ /w/ /ĭ/ /p/

mitt	**omit**	**omitted**	**you**	**hue**	**human**
/m/ /ĭ/ /t/	/ō/ /m/ /ĭ/ /t/	/ō/ /m/ /ĭ/ /t/ /ĭ/ /d/	/yū/	/h/ /yū/	/h/ /yū/ /m/ /ĭ/ /n/

it	**why**	**quiet**	**cue**	**cupid**
/ĭ/ /t/	/wh/ /ī/	/k/ /w/ /ī/ /ĭ/ /t/	/k/ /yū/	/k/ /yū/ /p/ /ĭ/ /d/

ray	**gray**	**gravy**	**age**	**agent**
/r/ /ā/	/g/ /r/ /ā/	/g/ /r/ /ā/ /v/ /ē/	/ā/ /j/	/ā/ /j/ /ĭ/ /n/ /t/

fix	**prefix**	**prefixes**	**jest**	**digest**
/f/ /ĭ/ /k/ /s/	/p/ /r/ /ē/ /f/ /ĭ/ /k/ /s/	/p/ /r/ /ē/ /f/ /ĭ/ /k/ /s/ /ĭ/ /z/	/j/ /ĕ/ /s/ /t/	/d/ /ī/ /j/ /ĕ/ /s/ /t/

ick	**Rick**	**trick**	**tricks**	**matrix**
/ĭ/ /k/	/r/ /ĭ/ /k/	/t/ /r/ /ĭ/ /k/	/t/ /r/ /ĭ/ /k/ /s/	/m/ /ā/ /t/ /r/ /ĭ/ /k/ /s/

free	**went**	**frequent**	**frequently**
/f/ /r/ /ē/	/w/ /ĕ/ /n/ /t/	/f/ /r/ /ē/ /k/ /w/ /ĕ/ /n/ /t/	/f/ /r/ /ē/ /k/ /w/ /ĕ/ /n/ /t/ /l/ /ē/

Phonemic Awareness Activities (Continued)

3. **Substitution Task** Substitute the first sound with the second sound to make a new word.

   stupid /ĭd/ – /er/   **solo** /s/ – /p/   **agent** /ā/ – /er/   **tiny** /n/ – /d/

   voter /v/ – /m/   **glider** /g/ – /s/   **soda** /d/ – /f/   **recent** /r/ – /d/

4. **Sound Reversals** Reverse the sounds (phonemes) to make a new word or words (**pit – tip**).

   Max – scam   basic – kiss Abe   focus – sick oaf   toga – a goat

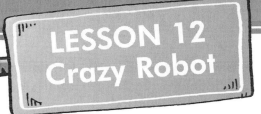

Dictate words in the lesson word list for Pretest and Posttest administration. Modify the number of words as needed.

Lesson 12 Word List

1. shady
2. solo
3. tiny
4. equip
5. crazy
6. omit
7. human
8. Venus
9. quiet
10. cupid
11. gravy
12. robot
13. climax
14. equal
15. humid
16. agent
17. rechecked
18. moment
19. prefixes
20. digested
21. matrix
22. prejudge
23. restitched
24. frequently

Irregular words: other than, friend, something, build, heart

Spelling Concept: The **open syllable** and long vowels.

This week's spelling words have **open syllables** that end with **single vowels**. These single vowels sound **long**. Single vowels make their long sound when they are happy and free. Because the vowel is at the end of an open syllable, there is no consonant guard to keep that vowel prisoner in the drafty, dank, and dastardly dungeon where guarded vowels sit sad and muffled. Vowels can escape! Wouldn't you be happy to escape from the dungeon? Vowels are free at the syllable's end to sing their names. When a vowel sings its name, we call that its **long** sound.

There is one exception: the letter **y** sings the names of *other* vowels, usually /ē/ and /ī/.

In these words, the syllable break happens right after the vowel letter that sings its name (its long vowel sound). Notice that **y** sings the long sounds /ē/ and /ī/.

ba–by

cri–sis

ro–bot

e–ven

ha–lo

Ju–ly

Underline the vowel letters in this lesson's words that represent long vowel sounds (that say their letter name). Do not include the irregular words, but do include y if it sings another vowel's name. Then, sort the words according to their long vowel sounds. Put a star (★) next to words that fit in more than one group.

Lesson 12 Word List

1. sh<u>a</u>d<u>y</u>
2. s<u>o</u>l<u>o</u>
3. t<u>i</u>n<u>y</u>
4. <u>e</u>qu<u>i</u>p
5. cr<u>a</u>z<u>y</u>
6. <u>o</u>mit
7. h<u>u</u>man
8. V<u>e</u>nus
9. qu<u>i</u><u>e</u>t
10. c<u>u</u>p<u>i</u>d
11. gr<u>a</u>v<u>y</u>
12. r<u>o</u>bot

13. cl<u>i</u>max
14. <u>e</u>qual
15. h<u>u</u>mid
16. <u>a</u>gent
17. r<u>e</u>checked
18. m<u>o</u>ment
19. pr<u>e</u>fixes
20. d<u>i</u>gested
21. m<u>a</u>trix
22. pr<u>e</u>judge
23. r<u>e</u>stitched
24. fr<u>e</u>quentl<u>y</u>

Irregular words: other than, friend, something, build, heart

/ā/ (as in grape)	/ē/ (as in me)	/ī/ (as in like)	/ō/ (as in hose)	/ū/ or /yū/ (as in suit or huge)
sha-dy ★	e-quip	ti-ny ★	so-lo	hu-man
cra-zy ★	Ve-nus	qui-et	o-mit	cu-pid
gra-vy ★	e-qual	cli-max	ro-bot	hu-mid
a-gent	re-checked	di-gest-ed	mo-ment	(super)
ma-trix	pre-fix-es	(pilot)	(total)	(noodle)
(aphid)	pre-judge	(lilac)	(modem)	(unit)
(table)	re-stitched	(Irish)		
	fre-quent-ly			
	sha-dy ★			
	ti-ny ★			
	cra-zy ★			
	gra-vy ★			
	(read)			
	(before)			

Now, go back and divide the words into syllables. Add two new words with open syllables to each group and circle these new words.

Example answers are circled above.

Exercise 2

Scavenger Hunt Have lots of fun navigating this five-part exercise! All of the questions relate to the words in this lesson's word list (excluding the irregular words).

Lesson 12 Word List

1. shady	7. human	13. climax	19. prefixes
2. solo	8. Venus	14. equal	20. digested
3. tiny	9. quiet	15. humid	21. matrix
4. equip	10. cupid	16. agent	22. prejudge
5. crazy	11. gravy	17. rechecked	23. restitched
6. omit	12. robot	18. moment	24. frequently

Irregular words: other than, friend, something, build, heart

a. **Open-ended syllables:** List the six words in this lesson's word list that end in an open syllable with a long vowel sound.

solo   shady   tiny

crazy   gravy   frequently

Five of these words end with the letter __y__ , which represents the / $\bar{e}$ / sound.

b. **Special /k/:** List the four words that use the **qu** spelling to represent the /kw/ sound. Then, underline the **qu** letters.

<u>qu</u>ip   <u>qu</u>iet

e<u>qu</u>al   fre<u>qu</u>ently

Now, list the three words that use the **x** spelling to represent the /ks/ combination. Underline each **x** letter.

clima<u>x</u>   prefi<u>x</u>es   matri<u>x</u>

c. **Blender:** Box the other consonant blends (not **qu**) in your study words. Then, list the words you found that have consonant blends.

[cr]azy	[gr]avy	[cl]imax
age[nt]	mome[nt]	dige[st]ed
ma[tr]ix	re[st]itched	freque[nt]ly

Pick three consonant blends from the words above and list them here.
Then, in four minutes, list as many new words as you can with these consonant blends.
Answers will vary.

d. **Openings:** Underline the vowel letters in these words that represent long vowel sounds.

shady   solo   tiny   equip

crazy   omit   human   Venus

How many long vowel sounds are in these words? __12__

Show where the syllables divide—after the vowel in the open syllable—by scooping under the syllables. Note that a syllable may be only one letter if it represents a long vowel sound.

e. **Di-ing and Tri-ing:** Two of your study words have digraphs, and two others have trigraphs. List these four words and underline the digraphs and trigraphs in them.

shady   rechecked   prejudge   restitched

Spelling Concept: Adding the past tense suffix.

Mr. Ed As you have learned, the **-ed** suffix is added to verbs (action words) to show that the action took place in the past. We call these verbs **past tense** verbs. The **-ed** suffix is tricky to spell because it can sound three different ways:

bang**ed** – /d/   snack**ed** – /t/   lift**ed** – /id/

Only in the last example is the **-ed** a whole new syllable with a sounded vowel.

Add the suffix -ed to these words. Then, sort the words based on the sound the **-ed** suffix represents.

open*ed*   equal*ed*   digest *ed*   solo *ed*   frequent *ed*

prevent *ed*   recheck *ed*   label *ed*   restitch *ed*   quiet*ed*

/d/ (as in **banged**)	**/t/** (as in **snacked**)	**/id/** (as in **lifted**)
o-pened	*re-checked*	*di-gest-ed*
e-qualed	*re-stitched*	*fre-quent-ed*
so-loed		*pre-vent-ed*
la-beled		*qui-et-ed*

Scoop under the syllables in each of the words you have just listed.

(Only the words in the right-hand column add a new spoken syllable when **-ed** is added. The others have an *inflectional morpheme*—a meaningful part—that makes only a single consonant sound.)

Spelling Concept: Wishy Y Many words that end with the letter **y** are **adjectives** (words that describe nouns) in which the **y** is a suffix. The **-y** suffix means "the state or quality of."

Fill in the blanks with a noun that each **-y** adjective could describe. An example is provided to help you get started. *Example answers:*

	What?		What?		What?
tidy	_cabin_	holy	_cow_	puny	_amount_
shady	_campus_	crazy	_person_	tiny	_gymnast_
icy	_storm_	lazy	_bum_		

Spelling Concept: Totally -ly The **-ly** suffix is added to words that describe verbs. Words that end in **-ly** and that describe verbs are called **adverbs**.

Add the -ly ending to these words to make adverbs. Then, give a verb (action word) that each adverb could describe. An example is provided to help you get started. *Example answers:*

	Did what?		Did what?
open _ly_	_complained_	vacant _ly_	_stared_
secret _ly_	_rechecked_	equal _ly_	_split_
even _ly_	_stitched_	total _ly_	_divided_
tender _ly_	_held_	quiet _ly_	_sneaked_

Spelling Concept: PREfix Review Two common prefixes, <u>re-</u> and <u>pre-</u>, are open syllables ending with the single vowel <u>e</u>.

> <u>re-</u> means "back or again"   <u>pre-</u> means "before."

Exercise 6

Build as many words as you can by adding the prefixes <u>re-</u> and <u>pre-</u> to these roots or base words. Then, use two of the words you have built in sentences that demonstrate their meanings.

> copy   fill   judge   fix   hang   chill   test

Example answers:

<u>re-</u> ("back or again")   <u>pre-</u> ("before")

recopy   refill   prefill   prejudge

refix   rehang   prefix   pretest

rechill   retest   prechill   _____

Answers will vary.

_____

_____

_____

_____

_____

_____

_____

Reading and Spelling Concept: Alternative **vowel-consonant-vowel (<u>vcv</u>)** syllable division.

In most of your study words this week, there is a single consonant stuck between two long vowels that you can sing. This exposed position drives the lone consonant crazy! Consonants are happier when they're with other consonants. When consonant letters are stuck alone between two vowels, they can get confused. Sometimes, they run right into the front of the second syllable. Of course, the first vowel is happy when the lone consonant guard runs away, because the vowel is then free to sing its name.

Some consonants are more reliable and trustworthy, however, and they stay to guard the first vowel. In this case, the first syllable stays closed and guarded, and the vowel stays stuck in the dungeon—sad, grumpy, and sounding short. Notice the contrasting vowel sounds of each syllable in the following word pairs:

li–lac / lim–bo   me–ter / met–al   ma–jor / mag–ic

Exercise 7

In each of these word pairs, underline the first syllable if it is open (with a long vowel sound), and box the first syllable if it is closed (with a short, guarded vowel sound).

<u>ma</u>jor / magic   <u>li</u>lac / limit   timid / <u>ti</u>dy

<u>ri</u>val / river   color / <u>co</u>lon   finish / <u>fi</u>nal

<u>pu</u>ny / punish   proper / <u>pro</u>pel   <u>fe</u>ver / never

radish / <u>ra</u>dar   <u>e</u>ven / ever   visit / <u>vi</u>sor

Sentence Dictations Create six sentences that use each group of words. High-frequency, irregular words are underlined. After everyone shares their sentences with the class, choose the best of the bunch that your teacher can use for dictation sentences. Write the sentences and correct your own work immediately.

Example answers:

1. prejudge, <u>friend</u>, quiet *Don't prejudge my friend just because she is quiet.*

2. <u>something</u>, digested, gravy *I digested something in the gravy that wasn't happy to be there.*

3. frequently, agent, rechecked *The agent frequently rechecked his bookings.*

4. <u>other</u> <u>than</u>, human, robot *A robot is the only thing, other than a human, that would work.*

5. matrix, equal, <u>build</u> *We could build a matrix with equal squares to record the results.*

6. restitched, cupid, <u>heart</u> *After Cupid was done with me, Betsy Ross could have restitched the holes in my heart.*

Speed Read Time yourself on three different days reading the following story out loud. Record your time and number of errors.

Bess, the dog, lived with Professor Thunker and a lazy cat named Tiger. Tiger was a tiny cat with tiger fur and an evil glint in her topaz eyes. Being a feline, Tiger felt that canines and humans were crazy and stupid compared to cats. Bess watched Tiger relax in shady spots when she was hot, silently snatch rodents, and soberly digest them. On this basis, Bess felt that Tiger was a demon, and she was totally scared of her. Wouldn't you be?

	Day 1	Day 2	Day 3
Time:	_____	_____	_____
Errors:	_____	_____	_____

Challenge Activity
How many open syllables can you find in this story? _43_

Finally: Take the Posttest, and record your score here. **Number Correct:** _____

LESSON 13
Rude Ape

Phonemic Awareness Activities

1. **Identify the Vowel Sound** Locate each vowel sound on the Vowel Sounds Chart.

brave /ā/   theme /ē/   stripe /ī/   slope /ō/   cube /yū/

twice /ī/   crate /ā/   quote /ō/   flute /ū/   these /ē/

use /yū/   prune /ū/   froze /ō/   strip /ĭ/   stretch /ĕ/

fine /ī/   fin /ĭ/   phone /ō/   fan /ă/   fed /ĕ/

2. **Segmentation Activity** Hold up the number of fingers—or show the number of markers—that is equal to the number of sounds (phonemes) in each of these words.

rave	brave	rip	ripe	stripe	strap	strapped
/r/ /ā/ /v/	/b/ /r/ /ā/ /v/	/r/ /ĭ/ /p/	/r/ /ī/ /p/	/s/ /t/ /r/ /ī/ /p/	/s/ /t/ /r/ /ă/ /p/	/s/ /t/ /r/ /ă/ /p/ /t/

lop	lope	slope	sloped	cub	cube	cubed
/l/ /ŏ/ /p/	/l/ /ō/ /p/	/s/ /l/ /ō/ /p/	/s/ /l/ /ō/ /p/ /t/	/k/ /ŭ/ /b/	/k/ /yū/ /b/	/k/ /yū/ /b/ /d/

ice	twice	at	ate	rate	crate	crated
/ī/ /s/	/t/ /w/ /ī/ /s/	/ă/ /t/	/ā/ /t/	/r/ /ā/ /t/	/k/ /r/ /ā/ /t/	/k/ /r/ /ā/ /t/ /ĭ/ /d/

Lou	lute	flute	row	rose	froze	frozen
/l/ /ū/	/l/ /ū/ /t/	/f/ /l/ /ū/ /t/	/r/ /ō/	/r/ /ō/ /z/	/f/ /r/ /ō/ /z/	/f/ /r/ /ō/ /z/ /ĭ/ /n/

CAMP CONSONANT

M.P.

3. **Deletion Task** Say each word after deleting the identified sounds (phonemes).

brave without /b/	**crate** without /k/	**froze** without /f/	**crate** without /r/
black without /l/	**spite** without /p/	**slave** without /l/	**smile** without /s/
pride without /p/	**frame** without /r/	**graze** without /r/	**scale** without /k/

4. **Substitution Task** Substitute the first sound with the second sound to make a new word.

stripe /ī/ – /ă/	**slop** /ŏ/ – /ō/	**brave** /b/ – /g/	**cube** /yū/ – /ŭ/
slope /ō/ – /ĭ/	**prime** /ī/ – /ĭ/	**shake** /ā/ – /ă/	**brake** /ā/ – /ō/
rack /ă/ – /ā/	**hop** /ŏ/ – /ō/	**pine** /ī/ – /ĭ/	**dim** /ĭ/ – /ī/

5. **Sound Reversals** Reverse the sounds (phonemes) to make a new word (**pit** – **tip**).

lope – pole	ape – pay	male – lame	face – safe
scale – lakes	lime – mile	file – life	knife – fine
dire – ride	sign – nice	dice – side	note – tone

Dictate words in the lesson word list for Pretest and Posttest administration. Modify the number of words as needed.

Lesson 13 Word List

1. brave	13. slope
2. cube	14. quote
3. flute	15. useful
4. ignite	16. froze
5. theme	17. confuse
6. twice	18. behave
7. these	19. recede
8. backbone	20. prune
9. stripe	21. reuse
10. crate	22. basement
11. locate	23. extreme
12. spruce	24. recline

Spelling Concept: The "magic <u>e</u>" syllable.

For years, people (or at least teachers) have been telling you that there is a "magic <u>e</u>" that uses its power to make a long vowel sound in the vowel letter two letters before it. (Some people believe that <u>e</u> bonks the vowel before it with a magic mallet, causing the vowel to squeal in pain!)

mād<u>e</u>	pīp<u>e</u>	frōz<u>e</u>
scēn<u>e</u>	fūs<u>e</u>	rūd<u>e</u>

Teachers have wanted to help you by not clogging your ears with the true, but murkier, explanation. The truth is that vowels and consonants are not the same. They're like cats and dogs. Sometimes they understand each other and sometimes they don't. Dogs think that cats are flighty, and cats think that dogs are just plain dumb. They're both right in some ways. Anyway, the vowels thought that if the English language were taken over by guarded, closed syllables, then the consonants would rule. Vowels would always be guarded. This made the vowels upset, and they met together to try and find a way to stop the consonants from achieving world domination.

The vowels decided to gang up on the single consonants that were sometimes left alone between vowels. You studied such <u>vcv</u> (vowel-consonant-vowel) words in Lesson 12—Crazy Robot. Many of these words had open syllables that formed when

the second greedy vowel pulled the one confused consonant guard its way, leaving the first vowel free to escape through the dungeon door and sing its name. You also saw that sometimes the guard ignored the second greedy vowel and stayed on duty, keeping the first vowel in the dungeon. (Take *that*, you sniffling vowel!)

Consonant Guard ON duty

sec–ond   van–ish   cop–y   mel–on

Consonant Guard OFF duty

ho–tel   fi–nal   ro–dent   mu–sic

Although the vowels felt as if this was a good start, they wanted something better, where the vowel would go free more often. They needed some way to pull the lone consonant guard away from the dungeon door more than half the time. The Fowl Fellowship Council gathered to scheme, plot, eat, and talk for days and daze. Finally, from their great stupor came great wisdom and a plan so clever that many believed the consonants would never know what hit them.

The council decision was to have a contest to determine which vowel could be the most friendly. The council members figured that a friendly vowel could get the guard talking and fooling around and distract it from its job. (This never happens to you, does it, dear student?) This way, the consonants couldn't accuse the vowels of bad intentions. After all, the vowels were only going to act friendly. What would be wrong with that?

The key to this plan, of course, was to find a vowel so personable, so mellow, so funny, and so cool that most consonants couldn't possibly ignore it. Vowels are natural show-offs, anyway. Each of the vowels thought that it was the slickest, goofiest, warmest, and finest and that it would be the one chosen to be this sly, goodwill ambassador.

The council decided on a contest with the following rules:

1. The winner would be the vowel that the council judged to have the best vibes overall.

2. The winner would have the privilege and responsibility of carrying out the following duties:
   - Distract the consonant guard standing behind it with funny faces and other pleasantries.
   - Guard the back door to make sure no new consonants come in.

Because these duties themselves were felt to be so burdensome and so important—and to save energy—it was agreed that the chosen vowel would do its job in silence. All the vowels agreed to this, since it seemed fair (and sneakiest) to all. This way, the vowels that didn't win would still be better off because they would have a better chance of being free. They could sing out their beautiful names more often, even if they didn't get used as much as the chosen vowel.

All the vowels were nervous on the day of the contest. **O** got up first and sang its low sound, which was like a foghorn on a drizzly night. The judges noticed that **O**'s mouth was very round, like yours might be if you ate a lemon. **I** came next and sang a beautiful, piercing, haunting song. The judges were again distracted, however, because **I**'s mouth quivered and ended up looking like a snarling dog (and we know how the vowel cats felt about dogs). When **I** was done, **U** got up and sang another wavering song that was mellow, like an echo. Again, the judges couldn't help but notice a peculiarity: **U** moved its mouth inward, like the return wave from **I**. **U** ended up with the lemon face, which soured everyone's mood.

A did a bit better; its sound was steady, if not spectacular, and the judges felt relieved that there was at least one vowel that could possibly do the job. All eyes (and **I**'s) then fell on **E**, the last vowel to audition. **E** sang out a clear song, like a bell. All the other vowels were enraptured by the sound. When the judges looked at **E**, they saw a smile that radiated out at them with such strength and brilliance that they had to smile back.

So, **E** was chosen, and the plan worked wonderfully. The vowels got their way without being bossy, and the consonants never realized what happened; because they enjoyed the company of **E** so much, they left vowels unguarded like crazy. Vowel names were ringing out in love songs and poems. In the words of sports announcers and meteorologists, "It was *awesome*!"

This week, you will get to see this wonderful cast of characters in action as we delve into the wonders of the vowel-consonant-silent -**e** (**vc** + silent -**e**) syllable.

Reminder: What are the two tasks **E** is responsible for?

1. Distract the consonant guard standing behind it with funny faces and other pleasantries.

2. Guard the back door to make sure no new consonants come in.

Spelling Concept: The **e** Sign.

This week's words all have **vc +** silent **-e syllables**: a single, long vowel followed by a consonant and a silent, "magic **e**." This silent **e** marks or signals that the preceding vowel is long-sounding.

The final silent **e** is rumored to have possession of a hammer that it uses to bonk the single vowel before it on the head. The surprised single vowel then yells out its name (long sound) in pain. However, you now know the true story; you know that vowels (especially **e**) are peaceful and friendly, but shrewd.

Make a cartoon character of each vowel. Locate each vowel sound on the Vowel Sounds Chart from Lesson 11—Valley of the Vowels. Draw each cartoon character with a face that matches the way your mouth looks when you say each long vowel.

/ā/
(as in **Abe**)

/ē/
(as in **Eve**)

/ī/
(as in **Ike**)

/ō/
(as in **Rose**)

/ū/
(as in **Jude**)

/yū/
(as in **muse**)

Sort the words in this week's word list based on the long vowel sound in the <u>vc +</u> silent <u>-e</u> (or <u>vc + -e</u>) syllables.

Lesson 13 Word List

1. brave	9. stripe	17. confuse
2. cube	10. crate	18. behave
3. flute	11. locate	19. recede
4. ignite	12. spruce	20. prune
5. theme	13. slope	21. reuse
6. twice	14. quote	22. basement
7. these	15. useful	23. extreme
8. backbone	16. froze	24. recline

Example answers have stars (★).

/ā/ (as in **Abe**)	/ē/ (as in **Eve**)	/ī/ (as in **Ike**)	/ō/ (as in **Rose**)	/ū/ (as in **Jude**)	/yū/ (as in **muse**)
brave	theme	ignite	backbone	flute	cube
crate	these	twice	slope	spruce	useful
locate	recede	stripe	quote	prune	confuse
behave	extreme	recline	froze	crude ★	reuse
basement	scene ★	while ★	broke ★	June ★	mule ★
chase ★	eve ★	stride ★	grove ★	include ★	refuse ★
blame ★	compete ★	sunshine ★	tadpole ★	costume ★	compute ★
cascade ★	supreme ★	recite ★	postpone ★	fluke ★	huge ★

Now, go back and add new words to each group. Star (★) the words that you add.

Spelling Concept: Review of three syllable types.

Because you are becoming word-smart, you are now familiar with at least three kinds of syllables:

1. <u>vc +</u> silent <u>-e</u> **syllable**—a single vowel + a consonant + a silent <u>-e</u>: <u>**ape**</u>, <u>**eve**</u>, <u>**robe**</u>

2. **Open syllable**—ends with a single long vowel that is unguarded: **b<u>e</u>**, **h<u>o</u>–b<u>o</u>**, **b<u>a</u>–b<u>y</u>**

3. **Closed syllable**—a single short vowel + one or more consonant guards: **b<u>e</u>t**, **r<u>o</u>b**, **m<u>a</u>sk**

Mark the vowels in these words as long or short. Then, divide these words into syllables by scooping under each syllable. Finally, label each syllable type according to its number, as described above.

1. <u>vc +</u> silent <u>-e</u>	2. Open	3. Closed

lōcāte
2   1

ūsefŭl
1   3

cŏnfūse
3   1

behāve
2   1

ignīte
3   1

băckbōne
3   1

recēde
2   1

ūselĕss
1   3

rēūse
2   1

bāsemĕnt
1   3

ĕxtrēme
3   1

reclīne
2   1

Rewrite each of these words, ending them with a silent **-e**. Then, read each word in the pairs you have made.

at   _ate_   bit   _bite_   shin   _shine_

can   _cane_   cut   _cute_   hop   _hope_

cap   _cape_   hid   _hide_   them   _theme_

fad   _fade_   fat   _fate_   fin   _fine_

tub   _tube_   sit   _site_   hug   _huge_

gap   _gape_   rid   _ride_   rob   _robe_

plum _plume_   mad   _made_   slop   _slope_

shad _shade_   Tim   _time_   rag   _rage_

plan _plane_   cub   _cube_   mat   _mate_

Mix and match these syllables to make words.

Set 1:

re	ful
ig	cede
use	ume
vol	nite

recede

ignite

useful

volume

Set 2:

base	have
re	treme
ex	ment
be	cline

basement

recline

extreme

behave

Spelling Concept: Consonant blends.

What is a consonant blend?

A consonant blend is two or three consonant sounds before or after

a vowel in the same syllable.

Remember: A blend exists within a syllable, even though a word might have two or more syllables in it. For example, there is no blend in **backbone**. The **ck** is a **digraph**, and the **b** starts the second syllable all by itself.

Exercise
6

Underline all of the consonant blends in this lesson's word list. Can you find all 13? List three of the blends and use them to write as many other words as you can in four minutes.

Lesson 13 Word List

1. <u>br</u>ave	9. <u>str</u>ipe	17. confuse
2. cube	10. <u>cr</u>ate	18. behave
3. <u>fl</u>ute	11. locate	19. recede
4. ignite	12. <u>spr</u>uce	20. <u>pr</u>une
5. theme	13. <u>sl</u>ope	21. reuse
6. <u>tw</u>ice	14. quote	22. baseme<u>nt</u>
7. these	15. useful	23. ex<u>tr</u>eme
8. backbone	16. <u>fr</u>oze	24. re<u>cl</u>ine

Blend 1:

_____

_____

_____

_____

_____

_____

_____

_____

Blend 2:

_____

_____

_____

_____

_____

_____

_____

_____

Blend 3:

_____

_____

_____

_____

_____

_____

_____

_____

Answers will vary.

Now, build strings of rhyming words by filling in the blanks with consonant letters or consonant blends—including the ones that you circled and listed in Exercise #6. (An example is provided to help you get started.) Read your lists when you're done.

Example answers:

cr	ate	st	age	br	ace	cr	ave
sl	ate	w	age	pl	ace	gr	ave
pl	ate	c	age	sp	ace	br	ave
gr	ate	p	age	tr	ace	sl	ave
pr	ide	tw	ine	sl	ope	st	oke
br	ide	br	ine	gr	ope	br	oke
str	ide	sp	ine	sc	ope	sm	oke
sl	ide	sw	ine	h	ope	str	oke

Now, write a meaningful sentence using as many of your rhyming words as you can.

_____

_____

_____

_____

_____

_____

Answers will vary.

Spelling Concept: Crazy /z/ has several spellings.

The sound /z/ is a truly **CRA_Z_Y** pain to spell. When /z/ is at the end of a word, it is sometimes spelled with **s** (as in **has**, **was**, **his**, **as**, **is**, **does**) or **zz** after short vowels (as in **buzz**, **jazz**). When the plural sounds like /z/, it is still spelled with **s** (as in **dogs**).

After long vowels, the /z/ sound is more often spelled with **se**: **wise**, **these**, **those**, **fuse**

However, the letters **ze** are sometimes used instead: **gaze**, **doze**, **haze**, **froze**

Fill in the blanks with **s** or **z** to represent the /z/ sound.

amu_s_e   fro_z_e

re_s_ult   di_s_po_s_e

ga_z_e   ho_s_e

u_s_e   la_z_y

ro_s_e   mu_s_ic

si_z_e   cra_z_e

sunri_s_e   pri_z_e

expo_s_e   the_s_e

Exercise 9a

In the word **use**, the letter **s** can represent either the /z/ or the /s/ sound, depending on the meaning of the word. Write a sentence that uses the word **use** both ways. What does each word mean?

_____

_____

_____

_____

Example answers:

If you **use** (/z/) a pickle to whack your brother on the head, that **use** (/s/) is sour.

Always **use** (/z/) a pickle for its intended **use** (/s/): to make your sandwich soggy.

Use (/z/) is a verb meaning to put into action, to utilize, or to employ something.

Use (/s/) is a noun meaning how something is employed or applied.

Exercise 9b

Build new words by adding the following prefixes and suffixes to the root **use**. Underline the **s** if it sounds like /s/. Box the **s** if it sounds like /z/.

Prefixes

| re-   mis-   dis- |

reu[s]e _____

misu[s]e _____

disu[s]e _____

Suffixes

| -ful   -less |

u<u>s</u>eful _____

u<u>s</u>ele<u>ss</u> _____

_____

Spelling Concept: Word Construction Zone We build longer words in different ways, depending on where the word parts, or **morphemes**, come from.

Exercise 10

Compounding Your Problems Compound words come from the Anglo-Saxon language stream. You remember (of course) the three different ways that compound words can be formed. Give an example of each form here.

Example answers:

classmate   forty-five   White House

Here is a golden opportunity for you to measure your compounding skills (or how confounded you are). Remain calm! Start by building as many compound words as you can from these two base words. Write your words and total the number. Next, go to a dictionary and list any new compound words you find with these two base words. Record the number of new words you found. You have ten minutes, so get cracking!

Example answers:

base   **back**

baseball   backache

base hit   back away

basement   backbiting

base path   backbreaking

base runner   backcountry

baseboard   backfield

baseline   backfire

base pair   background

base pay   backhoe

base angle   backlog

_____   back out

_____   backseat

Your total: _____

Dictionary total: _____

Spelling Concept: Latin Lingo How Latin-based words are formed.

Latin-based words are built by combining word parts, called **morphemes**. These word parts include prefixes, roots, and suffixes. A root word, such as **form**, may be a common part in a large word family:

con**form**   in**form**   de**form**   un**form**ed

This lesson's spelling words use three Latin roots: **fuse** ("to pour"); **use** ("to use"); and **cede** ("to go"). Combine these roots with the appropriate prefixes below to build Latin-based words. Use each of these words in a sentence that demonstrates its definition.

Example answers:

Prefix   **Words**
re- ("back or again")   refuse   reuse   recede

I refuse to stuff that pickle up my nose.

We reuse spelling books by turning them into compost.

We all enjoy watching our teacher's hairline recede.

Prefix   **Words**
pre- ("before")   preuse   precede

The dealer will preuse the computer to be sure it works.

This introduction will precede the body of your report.

_____

Prefix   **Words**
com- / **con-** ("together or with")   confuse   concede

It is fun (and easy!) to confuse my students.

Herman had to concede the tennis match so that he could

get home in time to watch his favorite stupid cartoons.

Spelling and Usage Concept: Some words can be used as either nouns or verbs.

Nouns are _words that name persons, places, ideas, or things._

Verbs are _action, or doing, words._

Exercise 13

Each word listed can be used as either a noun or a verb. Circle two of these words and use them in sentences that show both usages. Label the word usage in the sentence as **N** (noun) or **V** (verb).

back   prune   crate   quote   spruce

Example answers:

	N/V
1. _My back itches because mosquitoes had a picnic there this morning._	N
I will back your idea by giving you all the money in your pocket.	V
2. _The fact that a prune is a dried plum doesn't stop me from eating them._	N
My wife likes to prune trees until all that is left is the stump.	V

Extreme Dictation First, work with a partner to create a short paragraph that uses at least 12 of this lesson's spelling words. Write about one of these topics: "Extreme Sports" or "Extreme Sorts" (sorts of people, animals, music, food, etc.). Your completed and corrected masterpieces can be used as dictation exercises for the rest of the class.

Lesson 13 Word List

1. brave	7. these	13. slope	19. recede
2. cube	8. backbone	14. quote	20. prune
3. flute	9. stripe	15. useful	21. reuse
4. ignite	10. crate	16. froze	22. basement
5. theme	11. locate	17. confuse	23. extreme
6. twice	12. spruce	18. behave	24. recline

Answers will vary.

Speed Read Time yourself on three different occasions reading the following sets of words out loud from top to bottom. Record your times in the box.

rip	tip	tub	at	lid
ripe	trip	cub	ate	Sid
stripe	strip	cube	plate	side
	stripe	tube	slate	slide
he				
hem	lop	ice	rat	cap
them	slop	nice	rate	cape
theme	slope	dice	crate	drape
		lice	grate	grape
us	use			
fuss	reuse	use	can	cod
fuse	misuse	useless	cane	code
confuse	misused	useful	crane	rode
refuse	overused	usefully		
infuse	underused	uselessly	rim	mad
infused			prim	made
confused			prime	fade

Day 1	Day 2	Day 3
Time: _____	Time: _____	Time: _____
Errors: _____	Errors: _____	Errors: _____

Finally: Take the Posttest, and record your score here. **Number Correct:** _____

LESSON 14
Silent E Meets Its End

Phonemic Awareness Activities

1. **Identify the Vowel Sound** Locate each vowel sound on the Vowel Sounds Chart.

hop /ŏ/	hope /ō/	punch /ŭ/	tap /ă/	tape /ā/
smart /ar/	quit /ĭ/	wet /ĕ/	slime /ī/	slim /ĭ/
cute /yū/	crude /ū/	scar /ar/	pitch /ĭ/	patch /ă/
stack /ă/	stock /ŏ/	peck /ĕ/	pick /ĭ/	puck /ŭ/

2. **Segmentation Activity** Hold up the number of fingers—or show the number of markers—that is equal to the number of sounds (phonemes) in each of these words.

limb	slim	slime	slimy	ape	shape	shaped
/l/ /ĭ/ /m/	/s/ /l/ /ĭ/ /m/	/s/ /l/ /ī/ /m/	/s/ /l/ /ī/ /m/ /ē/	/ā/ /p/	/sh/ /ā/ /p/	/sh/ /ā/ /p/ /t/

tap	tape	tapped	taped	slop	slope	sloped
/t/ /ă/ /p/	/t/ /ā/ /p/	/t/ /ă/ /p/ /t/	/t/ /ā/ /p/ /t/	/s/ /l/ /ŏ/ /p/	/s/ /l/ /ō/ /p/	/s/ /l/ /ō/ /p/ /t/

art	mart	smart	smarter	ache	rake	brake
/ar/ /t/	/m/ /ar/ /t/	/s/ /m/ /ar/ /t/	/s/ /m/ /ar/ /t/ /er/	/ā/ /k/	/r/ /ā/ /k/	/b/ /r/ /ā/ /k/

cub	cube	cubed	Cuban	ice	nice	twice
/k/ /ŭ/ /b/	/k/ /yū/ /b/	/k/ /yū/ /b/ /d/	/k/ /yū/ /b/ /ĭ/ /n/	/ī/ /s/	/n/ /ī/ /s/	/t/ /w/ /ī/ /s/

at	ate	crate	crated	rip	ripe	gripe
/ă/ /t/	/ā/ /t/	/k/ /r/ /ā/ /t/	/k/ /r/ /ā/ /t/ /ĭ/ /d/	/r/ /ĭ/ /p/	/r/ /ī/ /p/	/g/ /r/ /ī/ /p/

Phonemic Awareness Activities (Continued)

3. **Deletion Task** Say each word after deleting the identified sounds (phonemes).

smart without /s/   slimmer without /l/   smash without /s/   grace without /g/

smile without /s/   grim without /g/   flame without /f/   scare without /s/

4. **Substitution Task** Substitute the first sound with the second sound to make a new word.

hop /ŏ/ – /ō/   smart /m/ – /t/   punch /ŭ/ – /ĭ/   slim /ĭ/ – /ă/

rip /ĭ/ – /ī/   tape /ā/ – /ă/   slime /ī/ – /ĭ/   quit /ĭ/ – /ī/

pitch /ĭ/ – /ă/   stripe /ī/ – /ă/   grime /ī/ – /ĭ/   slime /s/ – /k/

5. **Sound Reversals** Reverse the sounds (phonemes) to make a new word (**pit – tip**).

limb – mill   taps – spat   mile – lime   stove – votes

nose – zone   choke – coach   stone – notes   case – sake

LESSON 14
Silent E
Meets Its End

Dictate words in the lesson word list for Pretest and Posttest administration. Modify the number of words as needed.

Lesson 14 Word List

1. hopped
2. smartest
3. punched
4. slimmer
5. taping
6. hopeless
7. quitting
8. shining
9. slimy
10. tapping
11. gripped
12. smashing
13. graceful
14. scaring
15. smiled
16. griping
17. thriving
18. pitched
19. scarring
20. sticking
21. grimy
22. grimmest
23. grinned
24. depleting

Exercise 1

Vowel Sound Awareness (auditory) As this week's roots or base words are read aloud, listen for the vowel sound and identify it on the Vowel Sounds Chart. (You can find the chart at the beginning of Lesson 11—Valley of the Vowels.) Say whether the sound is long, short, or something else. (There is one word that contains a **vc +** silent **-e** spelling whose sound is not on the Vowel Sounds Chart. Can you identify the word, sound it out, and write its sound combination?)

hop /ŏ/	smart /ar/	punch /ŭ/	slim /ĭ/
tape /ā/	grime /ī/	hope /ō/	quit /ĭ/
shine /ī/	slime /ī/	tap /ă/	grim /ĭ/
grip /ĭ/	smash /ă/	grace /a/	(scare /ār/)
smile /ī/	grin /ĭ/	gripe /ī/	thrive /ī/
pitch /ĭ/	scar /ar/	stick /ĭ/	deplete /ĭ/ /ē/

Sort this week's roots or base words (in Exercise #1) by their spelling patterns to match the column headings below. Look at the last two or three letters in each base word.

<u>vc + silent -e</u>	1 Vowel + 1 Consonant	2–3 Consonants
hope	hop	smart
gripe	grip	smash
thrive	quit	punch
shine	slim	pitch
grace	scar	stick
slime	tap	
scare	grin	
tape	grim	
smile		
grime		
deplete		

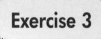

Alphabet Soup Write each set of words in alphabetical order.

a b c d e f g h i j k l m n o p q r s t u v w x y z

Set 1:

griping   grimmest   gripped graceful   grimy

1. graceful

2. grimmest

3. grimy

4. griping

5. gripped

Set 2:

scare smile stick slime shine scar smash smart slim

1. scar

2. scare

3. shine

4. slim

5. slime

6. smart

7. smash

8. smile

9. stick

Spelling Concept: Three rules for adding endings. These look familiar, we hope!

1. **Silent -e Rule**—When a root or base word ends with a silent **-e**:
   a. **Drop the -e** before adding an ending that starts with a *vowel*.
   b. **Keep the -e** before adding an ending that starts with a *consonant*.

2. **Doubling Rule**—If a root or base word ends with 1 vowel + 1 consonant:
   a. **Double the consonant** if the ending starts with a *vowel*.
   b. **Do not double the consonant** if the ending starts with a *consonant*.

3. **2+ Consonant Rule**—No change is necessary (just add the ending) if the root or base word ends with *two or more consonants*.

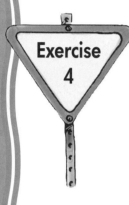

Exercise 4

Add the given endings to these words. Then, indicate which word-ending spelling rule you used. An example has been provided to help you get started.

use + ing =	using	1a	drip + ed =	dripped	2a
waste + ful =	wasteful	1b	fill + ed =	filled	3
hop + ed =	hopped	2a	grip + ing =	gripping	2a
hope + ed =	hoped	1a	gripe + ing =	griping	1a
hope + ful =	hopeful	1b	mope + ing =	moping	1a
quit + ing =	quitting	2a	mop + ing =	mopping	2a
quick + ly =	quickly	3	slim + er =	slimmer	2a
scar + ed =	scarred	2a	slime + y =	slimy	1a
scare + ed =	scared	1a	grace + ful =	graceful	1b
smash + ing =	smashing	3	thrive + ing =	thriving	1a

Exercise 5

Identify the base word and its ending in these words. Then, give the word-ending spelling rule that was used in adding the ending.

	Base word	Ending	Rule		Base word	Ending	Rule
sloppy	slop	y	2a	saving	save	ing	1a
slimy	slime	y	1a	mopped	mop	ed	2a
slapping	slap	ing	2a	sloping	slope	ing	1a

Use your knowledge of the word-ending spelling rules to fix the troubled spellings in this doggy tale about the ending of Professor Thunker's sandwich. Write the correct spellings above the misspelled words.

Exercise 6

Sandwich

The ~~Sand Which~~ Was There

Professor Thunker was ~~cuting~~ [cutting] a huge ~~peper~~ [pepper] and ~~smokeed~~ [smoked] bovine

snout sandwich in half when his cell phone ~~startted ringging~~ [started ringing]. Thunker ~~startted~~ [started]

~~taping~~ [tapping] his head, ~~hopping~~ [hoping] to remember where he last put the phone. ~~Suddennly~~ [Suddenly],

Thunker ~~droped~~ [dropped] his sandwich and went ~~runing~~ [running] upstairs. Thunker's ~~dogie wogie~~ [doggie woggie],

Bess, was ready for this. She ~~hoped~~ [hopped] up and went ~~raceing~~ [racing] to the kitchen

to ~~slober~~ [slobber] down the ~~overturnned~~ [overturned] sandwich. Bess was ~~waging~~ [wagging] her tail and

~~spiting~~ [spitting] out ~~peper~~ [pepper] parts when Thunker, ~~gripping~~ [griping] about telemarketers,

~~grimmly~~ [grimly] returned to see her ~~dinning~~ [dining] on his ~~diner~~ [dinner].

Challenge Activity How many spelling errors did you find? __25__

Underline the suffixes in this week's study words. Then, sort the words based on whether they can be used as a verb or as an adjective.

Lesson 14 Word List

1. hopp<u>ed</u>
2. smart<u>est</u>
3. punch<u>ed</u>
4. slimm<u>er</u>
5. tap<u>ing</u>
6. hope<u>less</u>
7. quitt<u>ing</u>
8. shin<u>ing</u>
9. slim<u>y</u>
10. tapp<u>ing</u>
11. gripp<u>ed</u>
12. smash<u>ing</u>
13. grace<u>ful</u>
14. scar<u>ing</u>
15. smil<u>ed</u>
16. grip<u>ing</u>
17. thriv<u>ing</u>
18. pitch<u>ed</u>
19. scarr<u>ing</u>
20. stick<u>ing</u>
21. grim<u>y</u>
22. grimm<u>est</u>
23. grinn<u>ed</u>
24. deplet<u>ing</u>

Verb		Adjective
hopped	quitting	graceful
scarring	shining	slimy
scaring	sticking	slimmer
punched	smiled	hopeless
tapping	griping	smartest
taping	gripped	grimy
thriving	grinned	grimmest
smashing	pitched	
depleting		

a. What suffixes did you find on verbs? _-ed, -ing_

b. What suffixes did you find on adjectives? _-ful, -y, -less, -er, -est_

Exercise 8

Sentence Dictations This week, we have a fabulous guest writer to write dictation sentences: **YOU!** Congratulations! This is a low-paying job with lots of fringe benefits. (We'll try to think of one.) In the meantime, write three sentences to use with your classmates. Each sentence should have at least two of this week's study words in it.

(**Note:** If you can use five or more study words in a single sentence—*that still makes sense to another human bean*—you can stop there.)

1. _____.

2. _____.

3. _____.

Speed Read Time yourself on three different days reading down this list of words out loud, one column at a time. Look for closed and open syllables. Remember, in two-syllable words with the **vccv** pattern, the first vowel is short-sounding (**hopping**); in <u>vcv</u> words, the first vowel is often long-sounding (**hoping**). Lots of people get tripped up on this! Record your time and errors in the box that follows the list.

hop	bit	grip	save
hope	bite	gripe	shave
hopping	bitter	gripping	shape
hoping	biter	griping	shaped
			shaping
slim	lick	slop	
slime	like	slope	hope
slimmer	licking	slopping	hopeful
slimy	liking	sloping	hopeless
			hoping
rip	scar	grim	hopping
ripe	scare	grime	hopped
ripping	scarring	grimmer	
riper	scaring	grimy	shin
			shine
star	cut	car	shiny
stare	cute	care	
starring	cutter	cars	rat
staring	cuter	cares	rate
			ratted
tap	fat	strip	rated
tape	fate	stripe	grated
tapping	fatter	strips	gated
taping	fated	stripes	fated

Day 1	Day 2	Day 3
Time: _____	Time: _____	Time: _____
Errors: _____	Errors: _____	Errors: _____

Finally: Take the Posttest, and record your score here. **Number Correct:** _____

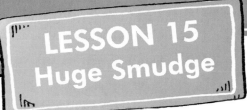

Phonemic Awareness Activities

1. **Identify the Vowel Sound** Locate each vowel sound on the Vowel Sounds Chart.

edge /ĕ/	lodge /ŏ/	cage /ā/	ridge /ĭ/	verge /er/
judge /ŭ/	stage /ā/	dodge /ŏ/	badge /ă/	ledge /ĕ/
sage /ā/	sledge /ĕ/	bridge /ĭ/	grudge /ŭ/	gorge /or/
plunge /ŭ/	large /ar/	rage /ā/	merge /er/	binge /ĭ/

2. **Segmentation Activity** Hold up the number of fingers—or show the number of markers—that is equal to the number of sounds (phonemes) in each of these words.

egg	edge	hedge	ledge	pledge	pledged
/ĕ/ /g/	/ĕ/ /j/	/h/ /ĕ/ /j/	/l/ /ĕ/ /j/	/p/ /l/ /ĕ/ /j/	/p/ /l/ /ĕ/ /j/ /d/

ran	rain	range	strange	stranger
/r/ /ă/ /n/	/r/ /ā/ /n/	/r/ /ā/ /n/ /j/	/s/ /t/ /r/ /ā/ /n/ /j/	/s/ /t/ /r/ /ā/ /n/ /j/ /er/

age	sage	stage	aged	caged	staged
/ā/ /j/	/s/ /ā/ /j/	/s/ /t/ /ā/ /j/	/ā/ /j/ /d/	/k/ /ā/ /j/ /d/	/s/ /t/ /ā/ /j/ /d/

in	bin	binge	you	hue	huge
/ĭ/ /n/	/b/ /ĭ/ /n/	/b/ /ĭ/ /n/ /j/	/yū/	/h/ /yū/	/h/ /yū/ /j/

rig	ridge	rage	range	grudge	grunge
/r/ /ĭ/ /g/	/r/ /ĭ/ /j/	/r/ /ā/ /j/	/r/ /ā/ /n/ /j/	/g/ /r/ /ŭ/ /j/	/g/ /r/ /ŭ/ /n/ /j/

3. **Deletion Task** Say each word after deleting the identified sounds (phonemes).

gage without first /g/	**pledge** without /p/	**bridge** without /b/	**plunge** without /p/
range without /n/	**sponge** without /j/	**grunge** without /n/	**binge** without /j/

Phonemic Awareness Activities (Continued)

4. **Substitution Task** Substitute the first sound with the second sound to make a new word.

sage /s/ – /p/	**ledge** /ĕ/ – /ŏ/	**fudge** /f/ – /b/	**edge** /j/ – /ch/
merge /m/ – /v/	**badge** /j/ – /ch/	**page** /p/ – /r/	**large** /l/ – /ch/

5. **Sound Reversals** Reverse the sounds (phonemes) to make a new word (**pit** – **tip**).

Jake – **cage**	**jay** – **age**	**ledge** – **jell**	**jab** – **badge**

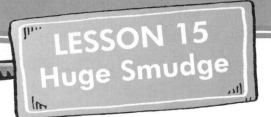

LESSON 15
Huge Smudge

Dictate words in the lesson word list for Pretest and Posttest administration. Modify the number of words as needed.

Lesson 15 Word List

1. dodge	13. verge
2. bulge	14. plunge
3. page	15. dredge
4. ridge	16. refuge
5. forge	17. smudge
6. huge	18. indulge
7. pledge	19. message
8. fringe	20. damage
9. judge	21. village
10. stage	22. knowledge*
11. largely	23. wreckage
12. cage	24. challenge

Irregular words: sought, by, of, some

* Marks a word that does not follow the pattern.

Spelling Concept: At the ends of words, the /j/ sound is spelled with **-dge** or **-ge**. In this lesson, we'll review the work we did with the **-dge** or consonant + **-ge** spellings in Lesson 10—Hodgepodge, plus add a few more wrinkles to the /j/ sound study and— hopefully— to your brain.

First of all, it is a spelling fact that no words in English end in a plain letter **j**. So spelling /j/ with a **j** is NOT an option. That leaves us with "soft **g**": a **g** followed by an **e** to represent the sound /j/.

Short vowels need extra protection if you add **-ge** after them. If you add **-ge** after a vowel, a "magic **e**" spelling results. For example, the word **wage** has a long vowel followed by **-ge**. To spell a short vowel before a /j/ sound, the **-ge** needs some help from a guardian that will keep the "magic **e**" far enough away. That's why we add a **-dge** after short vowels, unless there is already another consonant between the vowel and the **-ge**. The words in this week's spelling list have these patterns:

short **v** + **-dge** (r**idge**, d**odge**)	short **v** + **-nge** (fr**inge**, pl**unge**)
short **v** + **-lge** (b**ulge**, ind**ulge**)	**v** + **-r** + **-ge** (v**erge**, f**orge**)

Long vowels can be followed directly by **-ge**. The silent **e** is doing two jobs: it is representing the soft sound of **g** and it is marking the vowel as long:

long **v** + **-ge** (p**age**, h**uge**)

However, in multi-syllable words, the final syllable is often unaccented. This means that the silent **e** sometimes gets sleepy and doesn't mark the vowel. The vowel is then muffled into the *dreaded schwa* (ə) vowel sound. When words get longer, watch out for the schwa!

unaccented **v** + **-ge** = /əj/ (vill**age**, dam**age**)

Lesson 15 • *Huge Smudge* **57**

Phoneme Substitution and Deletion Create word magic by following these instructions.

Say **dot**. Change the /t/ to /j/.   Say **forge**. Change the /j/ to /s/.

Say **batch**. Change the /ch/ to /j/.   Say **verge**. Change the /j/ to /s/.

Say **refuge**. Change the /j/ to /s/.   Say **large**. Change the /j/ to /k/.

Say **wreckage**. Change the /j/ to /n/.   Say **strange**. Say it without the /j/.

Mark the vowels in these words from this lesson's study list as long (**L**), short (**S**), **v + -r** (**R**), or silent (**/**) (a diagonal line).

S /	R /	S /	R /	S /	L /
dodge	forge	judge	verge	smudge	page

S /	L /	L /	S /	S S /	L /
bulge	huge	stage	plunge	indulge	cage

S /	R / L	S /	S /	S /
pledge	largely	dredge	ridge	fringe

These words also have schwa vowels. Mark the vowels as in Exercise #2a, and then underline the schwa vowels.

S /	S /
knowledge	challenge

S /	S /
message	damage

S /	S /
village	wreckage

Exercise 3

Sort this lesson's words based on the spelling patterns of the column headings. Then, underline the letters that spell the **v +** /j/ sequence.

Lesson 15 Word List

1. dodge	7. pledge	13. verge	19. message
2. bulge	8. fringe	14. plunge	20. damage
3. page	9. judge	15. dredge	21. village
4. ridge	10. stage	16. refuge	22. knowledge*
5. forge	11. largely	17. smudge	23. wreckage
6. huge	12. cage	18. indulge	24. challenge

Irregular words: sought, by, of, some

* Marks a word that does not follow the pattern.

-dge	-nge	-lge	-rge	-ge (1 syllable)	-ge (2 syllables)
dodge	fringe	bulge	forge	page	message
ridge	plunge	indulge	largely	huge	damage
pledge	challenge		verge	stage	village
judge				cage	wreckage
dredge					refuge
smudge					
knowledge					

Make whole words by filling in the blanks with **-dge**, **-nge**, **-rge**, **-lge**, **-ge**, **-tch**, **-nch**, **-rch**, or **-ch**. (The sky's the limit; consider more than just one ending.) Then, mark the vowels as short (**S**), long (**L**), **v + -r** (**R**), or silent (**/**) (a diagonal line).

Example answers:

le   S /   ledge

ra   L / L / S   range, rage, ranch

bi   S /   binge

ca   S   L /   catch, cage

fu   S /   fudge

sna   S   snatch

sco   S   R   scotch, scorch

bu   S / S / S   budge, bulge, bunch

ba   S / R / S   badge, barge, batch

tru   S /   trudge

hu   L / S   huge, hutch

sti   S   stitch

di   S   R /   ditch, dirge

ple   S /   pledge

fri   S / S /   fringe, fridge

wre   S   S   wretch, wrench

ste   S   stench

bra   S   branch

la   S   R /   latch, large

do   S /   dodge

ma   S   R   match, march

i   S   S   itch, inch

gru   S / S /   grudge, grunge

pa   L / S   R   page, patch, parch

hu   L / S   huge, hunch

to   R   torch

wi   S   S   witch, winch

we   S / S   wedge, wench

be   S   bench

la   S   R   latch, large

sta   L / R   stage, starch

tha   S   thatch

stre   S   stretch

ha   S   hatch

cha   L / R /   change, charge

whi   S   which

Spelling Concept: Drop the final **e** when vowel suffixes are added.

If a word ends in /j/ (**dodge**, **rage**) and the suffix starts with **e** (**-ed**, **-er**) or **i** (**-ing**), drop the **e** to add the suffix:

dodg**e** + **-ed** = dodg**ed**

rag**e** + **-ing** = rag**ing**

outrag**e** + **-ed** = outrag**ed**

damag**e** + **-ing** = damag**ing**

Add the -ing ending to these words and write the new spellings in the blanks.

bulge _bulging_

pledge _pledging_

stage _staging_

cage _caging_

smudge _smudging_

indulge _indulging_

forge _forging_

judge _judging_

plunge _plunging_

dredge _dredging_

challenge _challenging_

sponge _sponging_

Spelling Concept: The ge Complex If a word ending begins with any letter other than **e** or **i**, don't drop the **e** from **-ge** words. The word needs the **e** to keep the soft sound of **g**, which is /j/.

engagement	arrangement	damageable	knowledgeable

Exercise 6a

Add the given suffixes and write the new spellings in the blanks.

gorge + ous   _gorgeous_

age + less   _ageless_

outrage + ous   _outrageous_

arrange + ment   _arrangement_

huge + ly   _hugely_

knowledge + able   _knowledgeable_

dodge + ing   _dodging_

manage + able   _manageable_

Now, take the suffixes off each of these words, and write the base words in the blanks.

charging — _charge_

smudged — _smudge_

dredging — _dredge_

arrangement — _arrange_

bulging — _bulge_

plunger — _plunge_

staging — _stage_

wedged — _wedge_

damaged — _damage_

pledged — _pledge_

pager — _page_

largely — _large_

challenger — _challenge_

knowledgeable — _knowledge_

ageless — _age_

Alphabet Soup Put these two sets of words in alphabetical order.

a b c d e f g h i j k l m n o p q r s t u v w x y z

Set 1:

| dodge   cage   damage   bulge |
| challenge   dredge |

1. bulge

2. cage

3. challenge

4. damage

5. dodge

6. dredge

Set 2:

| stage   refuge   wreckage   smudge |
| village   plunge   verge   ridge   page |

1. page

2. plunge

3. refuge

4. ridge

5. smudge

6. stage

7. verge

8. village

9. wreckage

As you have seen, the **-age** suffix is often unaccented and pronounced in the muffled tone of the dreaded schwa (ə) rolled into the /j/ sound (as in **baggage**). The **-age** suffix is cool because it's French and because it has several meanings. Sort these words according to the different meanings the **-age** suffix gives to them. Star (★) any words that apply to two of the headings.

baggage	wreckage	Anchorage	stoppage
manage	village	luggage	passage
breakage	garbage	shortage	acreage
cottage	bandage	damage	forage

An action or process	A result of	A collection	A place
manage	breakage	baggage	passage
bandage	wreckage	garbage	Anchorage
forage	shortage	acreage ★	acreage ★
damage ★	stoppage	luggage	cottage
	damage ★		village

Now, go back and underline the nouns and box the verbs.

What do you find about most **-age** words?

Most words with an **-age** suffix are nouns.

Word Construction Zone Compounding is an Anglo-Saxon way of forming new words by combining shorter words. Compound words can be joined together (**himself**), separated (**White House**), or hyphenated (**dog-eat-dog**).

Stage Fright Congratulations! You are at the stage in life when it's just right for you to find compound words built with the word **stage**. List four of them here.

_____   _____

_____   _____

Example answers:

stagecraft

stagecoach

stage direction

stage-manage

stagehand

stage left

stage right

stagestruck

Sentence Dictations Study these five sentences, and be prepared to write them to dictation.

1. The pandas sought refuge in their cage after a largely uneventful day.

2. The wreckage of the huge *Titanic* hull rested undisturbed, on the verge of discovery.

3. Her dress was damaged by a large smudge of gravy.

4. Judge not unless you be judged.

5. Pockets bulging, the villager gave me some fresh grapes.

Speed Read This journal entry describes Professor Thunker's life among the natives in Anchorage. Speed-read this absolutely fascinating account out loud, and record your time and errors on three different days.

Strange Georgia

North of Anchorage—through a peaceful village, along a ridge, and over an aged arched bridge—sits a hermitage with a cottage. The cottage is perched beside Three Cow Gorge, named for the strange cow Georgia who lives there with the sage, Page. For a cow, Georgia is strangely arranged and about the size of the grange. Each sunrise, Page trudges to the barn and gives Georgia a huge hug. Georgia nudges Page gently with her bulging baggage. Page then indulges Georgia, feeding her tonnage of organic wheat and corn porridge. Since Georgia gorges on porridge, her poundage is outrageously outstanding. Standing outside the hermitage, I often spot that huge cow and the grungy dog Bess near the garbage, bingeing on compost. Page thinks this is funny and is glad there is less wastage at the hermitage along the ridge.

Day 1	Day 2	Day 3
Time:	Time:	Time:
_____	_____	_____
Errors:	Errors:	Errors:
_____	_____	_____

Challenge Activity
Underline all of the letter spellings for the /j/ sound in this passage. How many did you find?

_____55_____

Finally: Take the Posttest, and record your score here. **Number Correct:** _____

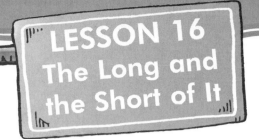

LESSON 16
The Long and the Short of It

Phonemic Awareness Activities

1. **Segmentation Activity** Hold up the number of fingers—or show the number of markers—that is equal to the number of sounds (phonemes) in each of these words.

elf	self	selfish	ax	lax	relax
/ĕ/ /l/ /f/	/s/ /ĕ/ /l/ /f/	/s/ /ĕ/ /l/ /f/ /i/ /sh/	/ă/ /k/ /s/	/l/ /ă/ /k/ /s/	/r/ /ē/ /l/ /ă/ /k/ /s/

aim	came	became	Gus	gust	disgust
/ā/ /m/	/k/ /ā/ /m/	/b/ /ē/ /k/ /ā/ /m/	/g/ /ŭ/ /s/	/g/ /ŭ/ /s/ /t/	/d/ /i/ /s/ /g/ /ŭ/ /s/ /t/

ran	ranch	branch	branches	crave	pave
/r/ /ă/ /n/	/r/ /ă/ /n/ /ch/	/b/ /r/ /ă/ /n/ /ch/	/b/ /r/ /ă/ /n/ /ch/ /ĭ/ /s/	/k/ /r/ /ā/ /v/	/p/ /ā/ /v/

ace	race	brace	bracelet	trait	frustrate
/ā/ /s/	/r/ /ā/ /s/	/b/ /r/ /ā/ /s/	/b/ /r/ /ā/ /s/ /l/ /ĭ/ /t/	/t/ /r/ /ā/ /t/	/f/ /r/ /ŭ/ /s/ /t/ /r/ /ā/ /t/

pet	Pete	compete	complete	completed
/p/ /ĕ/ /t/	/p/ /ē/ /t/	/k/ /ŭ/ /m/ /p/ /ē/ /t/	/k/ /ŭ/ /m/ /p/ /l/ /ē/ /t/	/k/ /ŭ/ /m/ /p/ /l/ /ē/ /t/ /ĭ/ /d/

2. **Deletion Task** Say each word after deleting the identified sounds (phonemes).

plate without /p/

glide without /l/

brace without /b/

self without /f/

branch without /b/

complete without /l/

brace without /r/

straight without /r/

brave without /b/

self without /s/

froze without /f/

stroke without /r/

Phonemic Awareness Activities (Continued)

3. **Substitution Task** Substitute the first sound with the second sound to make a new word.

shake /sh/ – /b/	**gave** /ā/ – /ĭ/	**rip** /ĭ/ – /ī/	**mope** /ō/ – /ŏ/
prim /ĭ/ – /ī/	**grip** /ĭ/ – /ā/	**kite** /ī/ – /ĭ/	**cod** /ŏ/ – /ō/
scrape /ā/ – /ă/	**quote** /ō/ – /ĭ/	**freeze** /ē/ – /ō/	**stroke** /ō/ – /ī/

4. **Sound Reversals** Reverse the sounds (phonemes) to make a new word (**pit** – **tip**).

side – **dice**	**Kate** – **take**	**safe** – **face**	**might** – **time**
cod – **dock**	**cots** – **stock**	**nip** – **pin**	**scene** – **niece**
pipe – **pipe**	**eke** – **key**	**stop** – **pots**	**lope** – **pole**

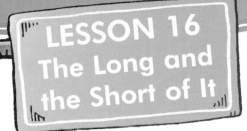

LESSON 16
The Long and the Short of It

Lesson 16 Word List

1. selfish
2. relax
3. became
4. lessons
5. disgust
6. respond
7. behave
8. donate
9. freshest
10. excite
11. combine
12. branches
13. pavement
14. dispute
15. conquest
16. inspire
17. frustrate
18. bracelet
19. complete
20. splendid
21. equal
22. complex
23. refinish
24. confuse

Irregular words: again, immune, because, where, useful, have been, too

Spelling Concept: Many two- and three-syllable words are combinations of open, closed, and <u>vc +</u> silent <u>-e</u> syllables. This lesson's word list contains only patterns you have already studied.

First, mark the vowel letters in this lesson's study words as long (L), short (S), silent (/), or schwa (ə). (Do not include the irregular words.)

Next, go back and divide the words into syllables by scooping under them (remember, every syllable has a talking vowel).

Finally, write the words in the sort columns. Underline the syllable that matches the heading. (Some words will apply to more than one column.)

Lesson 16 Word List

1. selfish (S S)
2. relax (L S)
3. became (L L /)
4. lessons (S ə)
5. disgust (S S)
6. respond (L S)
7. behave (L L /)
8. donate (L L /)
9. freshest (S ə)
10. excite (S L /)
11. combine (ə L /)
12. branches (S ə)
13. pavement (L / ə)
14. dispute (S L /)
15. conquest (S S)
16. inspire (S L /)
17. frustrate (S L /)
18. bracelet (L / ə)
19. complete (ə L /)
20. splendid (S S)
21. equal (L ə)
22. complex (S S)
23. refinish (L S ə)
24. confuse (ə L /)

Irregular words: again, immune, because, where, useful, have been, too

70   Spellography • A Student Road Map to Better Spelling

Closed syllable		Open syllable	vc + silent -e Syllable
self-ish	dis-gust	re-lax	be-came
les-sons	fresh-est	re-spond	do-nate
re-spond	com-bine	do-nate	com-bine
ex-cite	pave-ment	re-fin-ish	dis-pute
branch-es	con-quest	be-came	frus-trate
dis-pute	frus-trate	be-have	com-plete
in-spire	com-plete	e-qual	be-have
brace-let	e-qual		ex-cite
splen-did	re-fin-ish		pave-ment
com-plex			in-spire
con-fuse			brace-let
re-lax			con-fuse

Read down each column of syllables. Then, in each set, match a syllable in the first column with a syllable in the second column to make a word.

Example answers:

Set 1:

pave	lax	*pavement*
dis	spire	*dispute*
con	came	*conquest*
be	pute	*became*
in	quest	*inspire*
re	ment	*relax*

Set 2:

self	spond	*selfish*
dis	bine	*disgust*
do	have	*donate*
re	nate	*respond*
be	gust	*behave*
com	ish	*combine*

Syllables You Have Known Syllables are built around the vowel sound that lives in the syllable. **Closed** syllables arc dungeons that house weak, short vowel sounds. **Open** and <u>vc +</u> silent <u>-e</u> syllables usually have free, happy, long vowel sounds.

Three Bulls This week's study is built around a review of the three syllable types (**closed**, **open**, and <u>vc +</u> silent **-e**). Because the vowel <u>e</u> is such good company, it will lead you through a fascinating syllable review for your spelling pleasure.

Underline the syllable with the letter <u>e</u> in these words.

Exercise 3a

<u>e</u>vil   V<u>e</u>nus   r<u>e</u>play   z<u>e</u>bra   pr<u>e</u>fix

Name the type of syllable you underlined, and define it.

Open syllable, which ends with a single, unguarded vowel that usually sings its long sound.

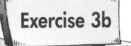
Exercise 3b

Underline the syllable with the letter <u>e</u> in these words.

<u>ed</u>it   b<u>egg</u>ar   str<u>etch</u>ing   in<u>tend</u>   sh<u>edd</u>ing

Name the type of syllable you underlined, and define it.

Closed syllable, which has a single vowel letter followed by one or more consonant guards. The vowel says its short sound.

Underline the syllable with the letter <u>e</u> in these words.

Exercise 3c

confus<u>e</u>   compl<u>ete</u>   disp<u>ute</u>   ump<u>ire</u>   tromb<u>one</u>

Name the type of syllable you underlined, and define it.

vc + silent -e syllable, in which the e is the silent marker that signals that the vowel before it sounds long.

Exercise 4

Divide into syllables the words in these similar word pairs. Use the vowel sounds to help decide if each syllable is open (ends in a vowel) or closed (ends in a consonant).

table / tablet	ta-ble	tab-let
puny / punish	pu-ny	pun-ish
secret / second	se-cret	sec-ond
local / topic	lo-cal	top-ic
rival / river	ri-val	riv-er
puppet / pupil	pup-pet	pu-pil
absent / able	ab-sent	a-ble
bonus / bonnet	bo-nus	bon-net
bacon / salad	ba-con	sal-ad
climax / limit	cli-max	lim-it
radar / radish	ra-dar	rad-ish
motto / motor	mot-to	mo-tor
polite / polish	po-lite	pol-ish
final / finish	fi-nal	fin-ish
profit / profile	prof-it	pro-file
music / musket	mu-sic	mus-ket
apple / apron	ap-ple	a-pron
fabric / fable	fab-ric	fa-ble
modest / rodent	mod-est	ro-dent
punish / tyrants	pun-ish	ty-rants

Exercise 5

Play "Syllable Concentration" using this lesson's study words broken into syllables. Start with 12 study words, including any you misspelled on the Pretest. Write each syllable on an index card. Mix the cards, and place them facedown in rows. The goal is to match syllables to create the study words.

Lesson 16 Word List

1. self–ish
2. re–lax
3. be–came
4. les–sons
5. dis–gust
6. re–spond
7. be–have
8. do–nate
9. fresh–est
10. ex–cite
11. com–bine
12. branch–es
13. pave–ment
14. dis–pute
15. con–quest
16. in–spire
17. frus–trate
18. brace–let
19. com–plete
20. splen–did
21. e–qual
22. com–plex
23. re–fin–ish
24. con–fuse

Say these syllables. Then, in the blanks next to them, write **C** for closed, **O** for open, or <u>**vc + -e**</u> for silent <u>**-e**</u> syllables.

gli	_O_	glid	_C_	glide	_vc + -e_
lid	_C_	frip	_C_	fripe	_vc + -e_
throt	_C_	throte	_vc + -e_	qui	_O_
quit	_C_	quite	_vc + -e_	quock	_C_
cho	_O_	chote	_vc + -e_	choke	_vc + -e_
scra	_O_				

Add whatever letters are needed to create a word using the kind of syllable indicated in the parentheses ( ).

Exercise 7

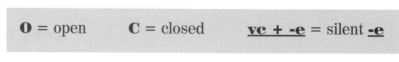
O = open	**C** = closed	<u>**vc + -e**</u> = silent <u>**-e**</u>

Example answers:

sh _e_ (**O**)	wh _ite_ (**vc + -e**)	qu _ick_ (**C**)	cr _y_ (**O**)
g _ave_ (**vc + -e**)	wh _o_ (**O**)	m _e_ (**O**)	cr _ate_ (**vc + -e**)
gr _ip_ (**C**)	th _ese_ (**vc + -e**)	str _ipe_ (**vc + -e**)	scr _ape_ (**vc + -e**)
gr _ape_ (**vc + -e**)	th _at_ (**C**)	d _ive_ (**vc + -e**)	sm _all_ (**C**)

Word Construction Zone Compounding is an Anglo-Saxon way of forming new words by combining shorter words. Compound words can be joined together (**himself**), separated (**White House**), or hyphenated (**dog-eat-dog**).

Self-concept Are you self-absorbed, self-aware, or even self-cleaning? What is your definition of the word **self** (<u>not</u> **shelf**)?

The essential and entire person different from all other persons in identity.

_____

Exercise 8b

Self-Evidence It's tricky to define the word **self** without using it in its own definition, don't you think? However, it's easy to find compound words built with **self**. To see if you get the self-concept—and to prove your self-worth as a self-respected collector of compound words—find and list at least five compound words (not yet mentioned) that use the word **self**.

_____   _____   _____

_____   _____   _____

Example answers:

self-absorbed	self-acting
self-assured	self-aware
self-centered	self-control
self-defense	self-help
self-image	self-made
self-pity	self-propelled
self-pride	self-regard
self-rule	

Befuddle! It's befuddling (and bewildering) how many Anglo-Saxon words use the prefix **be-**. It's also befuddling how many meanings **be-** has. So beware! Sort these **be-** words into two groups based on the meaning of the prefix in the word.

behind	belittle	before	behold	begin
befriend	befoul	bewitch	beside	

"near, around"

behind

beside

behold

before

_____

"to make; to treat"

bewitch

belittle

begin

befriend

befoul

Now, find and list five more **be-** words.

Exercise
9b

_____   _____

_____   _____

_____

Example answers:

becalm	begone	bejewelled	beneath
bedraggle	begrudge	belated	benign
become	befit	behalf	belief
betroth	bedazzle	befuddle	behave
below	between	beget	belabor
bemoan	betwixt		

Latin Word Construction Zone Words from the Latin language stream are built by adding **prefixes** and **suffixes** to **roots**. Some roots can stand alone as individual words (re**mark**ed), but many roots can make a word only if they combine with a suffix or a prefix (in**trude**).

Exercise 10a

In these words, box the prefixes, underline the roots, and circle the suffixes.

relax	freshest	confuse	disgust	bracelet
conquest	excite	refinish	branches	combine
dispute	pavement	complete	equal	

Exercise 10b

Like Ninja Turtles, some prefixes (such as **com-/con-** and **ex-/e-**) are mutants, with different spellings for the same prefix. In the spaces below, list both forms of these mutant prefixes. Also, choose one suffix from any word in Exercise #10a. Then, find three words in a dictionary that use each prefix and suffix form.

Example answers:

Prefixes		**Suffix**
com- / con-	ex- / e-	-est
complete	extreme	fastest
complex	exchange	slowest
concrete	eject	bravest

Word Yin-Yang Some words have **synonyms** and **antonyms**. The prefix <u>syn-</u> means "the same." The suffix <u>-nym</u> means "name." Synonyms are different words that have a common meaning, such as **fast/quick/speedy**. The prefix <u>anti-</u> means "the opposite." Antonyms are different words that have opposite meanings, such as **happy/sad** and **slim/stout**.

Exercise 11

Try not to become repulsed as you find three synonyms and three antonyms for the word **disgusting**.

Synonyms   Antonyms

_____   _____

_____   _____

_____   _____

Example answers:

Synonyms	Antonyms
revolting	attractive
nauseating	appealing
sickening	enticing
repugnant	charming
repellent	pleasing

Alphabet Soup Put these two sets of words in alphabetical order.

a b c d e f g h i j k l m n o p q r s t u v w x y z

Set 1:

| complete | combine | conquest |
| complex | confuse | |

1. combine _____

2. complete _____

3. complex _____

4. confuse _____

5. conquest _____

Set 2:

disgust	freshest	became
frustrate	branches	equal
dispute	behave	excite

1. became _____

2. behave _____

3. branches _____

4. disgust _____

5. dispute _____

6. equal _____

7. excite _____

8. freshest _____

9. frustrate _____

Magic Squares Create at least ten words from the letters in each magic square.

Magic Square

m	t	b
a	e	i
f	l	**FREE** consonant/ blend

_____

_____

_____

_____

_____

_____

_____

_____

_____

_____

Magic Square

d	s	ch
k	**FREE** vowel	t
f	h	m

_____

_____

_____

_____

_____

_____

_____

_____

Sentence Dictations With a partner, make up the best sentence you can with each of these groups of words. You can add endings if you need to. Irregular, high-frequency words are underlined. Then, help the class choose the five best sentences to use for dictation.

Example sentences:

1. **respond, frustrate, disgust, <u>again</u>** _If you respond again with disgust for his plan, you will frustrate Bert._

2. **behave, <u>immune</u>, dispute, <u>because</u>** _Because of the way you behave, you are immune to this dispute._

3. **relax, freshest, splendid, <u>where</u>** _Our splendid, relaxing pond is where you can locate the freshest water._

4. **refinish, lessons, <u>useful</u>, <u>have been</u>** _The lessons on how to refinish tables and chairs have been useful._

5. **selfish, combine, equal, <u>too</u>** _Curt was too selfish to combine his food with ours in an equal and fair way._

Speed Read Time yourself on three different days reading these columns of words out loud from top to bottom and left to right. (Remember: **open** and <u>vc +</u> silent <u>-e</u> syllables usually have free, long vowel sounds; **closed**, guarded syllables house sad, short vowel sounds.)

came	fat	even	become
fame	fate	ever	became
lame			behave
name	fin	bacon	behold
dame	fine	salad	behind
game	finish		before
same	final	Venus	befall
		venom	begin
ax	tub		belong
lax	tube	profile	bewilder
relax		profit	bewitch
relaxed	not		
	note	local	quest
Gus		topic	request
gust			conquest
disgust	pet	super	
disgusted	Pete	supper	spire
			perspire
	cut		inspire
Dave	cute	Polish	uninspire
rave		polish	
crave	slim		
save	slime	rival	dispute
saved		river	disputed
paved	din		
pavement	dine	climax	compute
	dinner	limit	computed
	diner		computer

Day 1	Day 2	Day 3
Time: _____	Time: _____	Time: _____
Errors: _____	Errors: _____	Errors: _____

Finally: Take the Posttest, and record your score here. **Number Correct:** _____

Phonemic Awareness Activities

1. **Segmentation Activity** Hold up the number of fingers—or show the number of markers—that is equal to the number of sounds (phonemes) in each of these words.

in	sin	cinch	inch	inched	inches
/ĭ/ /n/	/s/ /ĭ/ /n/	/s/ /ĭ/ /n/ /ch/	/ĭ/ /n/ /ch/	/ĭ/ /n/ /ch/ /t/	/ĭ/ /n/ /ch/ /ĭ/ /z/

each	leach	bleach	beach	beached	beaches
/ē/ /ch/	/l/ /ē/ /ch/	/b/ /l/ /ē/ /ch/	/b/ /ē/ /ch/	/b/ /ē/ /ch/ /t/	/b/ /ē/ /ch/ /ĭ/ /z/

inch	itch	ditch	ditches	dishes
/ĭ/ /n/ /ch/	/ĭ/ /ch/	/d/ /i/ /ch/	/d/ /ĭ/ /ch/ /ĭ/ /z/	/d/ /ĭ/ /sh/ /ĭ/ /z/

eke	week	squeak	squeaks	seeks	speaks
/ē/ /k/	/w/ /ē/ /k/	/s/ /k/ /w/ /ē/ /k/	/s/ /k/ /w/ /ē/ /k/ /s/	/s/ /ē/ /k/ /s/	/s/ /p/ /ē/ /k/ /s/

will	wheel	squeal	squeals	seals	steals
/w/ /ĭ/ /l/	/wh/ /ē/ /l/	/s/ /k/ /w/ /ē/ /l/	/s/ /k/ /w/ /ē/ /l/ /z/	/s/ /ē/ /l/ /z/	/s/ /t/ /ē/ /l/ /z/

cat	catch	snatch	snatched	pit	patch	patched
/k/ /ă/ /t/	/k/ /ă/ /ch/	/s/ /n/ /ă/ /ch/	/s/ /n/ /ă/ /ch/ /t/	/p/ /ĭ/ /t/	/p/ /ă/ /ch/	/p/ /ă/ /ch/ /t/

2. **Deletion Task** Say each word after deleting the identified sounds (phonemes).

ditch without /d/   **beach** without /b/   **branch** without /b/   **speech** without /s/

beach without /ch/   **grain** without /n/   **goal** without /l/   **roach** without /ch/

inch without /n/   **squeak** without /k/ /w/   **fleas** without /l/   **grains** without /r/

Phonemic Awareness Activities (Continued)

3. **Substitution Task** Substitute the first sound with the second sound to make a new word.

sneak /n/ – /p/	roach /ō/ – /ĭ/	catch /k/ – /p/	peach /p/ – /b/
leash /ē/ – /ă/	peach /ē/ – /ă/	catch /ă/ – /ō/	sweet /ē/ – /ĕ/
patch /p/ – /b/	punch /ŭ/ – /ĭ/	sheets /ē/ – /ŏ/	punch /p/ – /b/
bleach /ē/ – /ŏ/	flea /ē/ – /ū/	scratch /ă/ – /ē/	sheet /sh/ – /ch/

4. **Sound Reversals** Reverse the sounds (phonemes) to make a new word (**pit – tip**).

meet – team	patch – chap	seep – peace	lace – sail
stow – oats	reach – cheer	peak – keep	own – no
deal – lead	toe – oat	kneel – lean	May – aim

Dictate words in the lesson word list for Pretest and Posttest administration. Modify the number of words as needed.

Lesson 17 Word List

1. inches
2. beaches
3. ditches
4. fleas
5. goals
6. catches
7. roaches
8. grains
9. peaches
10. patches
11. sheets
12. branches
13. squeaks
14. punches
15. scratches
16. leashes
17. sneakers
18. bleachers
19. sketches
20. speeches
21. squelches
22. encroaches
23. squeals
24. tweezers

Irregular words:

of, where, were, their, worst

Spelling Concept: The plural of a noun, and sometimes the present tense of a verb, is made by adding either **-s** or **-es**. The ending that is added depends on the last sound of the base word or the root.

Phoneme and Morpheme Awareness As your teacher says these words, say the plural form aloud.

torch	elbow	boat	brush	gas	pail
flea	beet	tax	noise	face	arrow
peel	wrench	loan	day	spice	breeze
wish	mix	maid	tray	leak	glass

As your teacher says these words, take off the plural ending and say the base word.

benches	meats	reaches	tweaks	speakers
bleaches	batches	hunches	bleachers	witches
coaches	beets	thatches	wretches	shoals
trains	ranches	leashes	approaches	

Exercise 2a

Choose the correct plural ending to these words by adding **-s** or **-es**. Then, place each word in one of the two groups based on the way the plural version of the word is spelled and pronounced.

Lesson 17 Word List

1. inch	7. roach	13. squeak	19. sketch
2. beach	8. grain	14. punch	20. speech
3. ditch	9. peach	15. scratch	21. squelch
4. flea	10. patch	16. leash	22. encroach
5. goal	11. sheet	17. sneaker	23. squeal
6. catch	12. branch	18. bleacher	24. tweezer

-s (/s/, /z/)

squeaks	squeals
sheets	
fleas	
grains	
bleachers	
tweezers	
goals	
sneakers	

-es (/əz/)

inches	leashes
catches	squelches
patches	ditches
scratches	peaches
speeches	punches
beaches	sketches
roaches	encroaches
branches	

Note:

The plural **-s** sounds like /s/ when it follows consonant phonemes that are *unvoiced*, including /t/, /k/, /p/, /f/, and /th/ (as in **moths**).

The plural **-s** sounds like /z/ when it follows consonant phonemes that are *voiced*, including /d/, /b/, /g/, /v/, /th/ (as in **seethes**), /l/, /r/, /m/, /n/, and /ng/.

What rule or pattern can you find to tell you when to use **-es** (/əz/) to make a word plural? **Hint:** Listen to the last sound of the word.

Exercise 2b

_____

_____

_____

When singular words end with a sound that is produced by pushing a stream of air between your teeth—such as the /ch/ sound—you need an extra sound as a break between that hissing sound and the sound of the **s** in a plural ending. We use the letter **e** to represent a schwa sound as part of the **-es** plural spelling to separate these hissing sounds.

Spelling Concept: Vowel team syllables.

Many vowels are spelled with letter combinations. We have 15 vowel sounds in the English language, but only six vowel letters (<u>a</u>, <u>e</u>, <u>i</u>, <u>o</u>, <u>u</u>, and sometimes <u>y</u>), so they have to double up. The teams can stand for both long and short vowel sounds. Whenever a team of letters represents a vowel in a syllable, we call it a **vowel team syllable**. Some of these spellings are determined by the place of the vowel in the word; otherwise, they must just be learned from practice.

Exercise 3a

Sort this lesson's base words into one of the two given groups. (Do not use the irregular words.)

Lesson 17 Word List

1. inch	9. peach	17. sneaker
2. beach	10. patch	18. bleacher
3. ditch	11. sheet	19. sketch
4. flea	12. branch	20. speech
5. goal	13. squeak	21. squelch
6. catch	14. punch	22. encroach
7. roach	15. scratch	23. squeal
8. grain	16. leash	24. tweezer

Irregular words: of, where, were, their, worst

Vowel Team Words
(long vowel sound)

| | | **Single Vowel Words**
(short vowel sound) |

beach   roach   inch

goal   grain   patch

peach   sheet   punch

squeak   leash   sketch

sneaker   bleacher   catch

speech   encroach   branch

squeal   tweezer   scratch

flea   _____   squelch

_____   _____   ditch

Exercise 3b

In which column are the **-tch** and **consonant + -ch** words?
Underline those letter sequences.

Single vowel words (short vowel sound)

In which column are the **-ch** words? Underline those letter sequences.

Exercise 3c

Vowel team words (long vowel sound)

Alphabet Soup Write these eight spelling words in alphabetical order.

a b c d e f g h i j k l m n o p q r s t u v w x y z

squeaks	sneakers	squelches	sheets	scratches
	sketches	squeals	speeches	

1. scratches

2. sheets

3. sketches

4. sneakers

5. speeches

6. squeaks

7. squeals

8. squelches

Magic Squares Here are a pair of squares for your spelling pleasure. Race your classmates. How many words can you build in ten minutes using the letters in each square?

Magic Square

b	r	k
p	a ea e ee ea	ch
s	n	t

_____ _____
_____ _____
_____ _____
_____ _____
_____ _____
_____ _____
_____ _____
_____ _____

Word Total _____

Magic Square

qu	s	c
m	a ea e ee ea	r
t	FREE consonant diagraph	k

_____ _____
_____ _____
_____ _____
_____ _____
_____ _____
_____ _____
_____ _____
_____ _____

Word Total _____

Spelling Concept: Parts of speech.

All of these words from this lesson's word list can be used as both **nouns** (persons, places, things, ideas) and **verbs** (action or doing words):

inches	beaches	patches	ditches	sketches	branches
squeaks	catches	punches	scratches	squeals	leashes

Here's an example of how the word **seats** can be used as both a noun and a verb:
- The **seats** near the aisle were filled.   (**noun**)
- The theater **seats** fifty people.   (**verb**)

Exercise 6

Read this dramatic tale about the life of Clem. For the words in **bold** type: if the word is used as a noun, write the letter **n** above it; if the word is used as a verb, write the letter **v** above it; and if the word is used as an adjective, write the letter **a** above it.

Clem **fishes**. The **catch** Clem **catches squeaks** and **squeals** when

caught. The **squeaks** and **squeals** are heard by people on the **beaches** where

Clem **beaches** his skiff. Clem **ditches** the oars in a **ditch** under some

branches. By the **beach**, a stream **branches** in two where the **beached** boat

is **beached**. Clem eats what he **catches** and

sketches the **catch's** leftover parts. Clem works

on his **sketches** and **scratches**

scratches that **itch** only more

when Clem **scratches** them.

Exercise 7

Choose five of these words and write sentences for each of them that show how the word can be used as a **noun** and as a **verb**. Underline the noun usages, and box the verb usages.

inches	beaches	patches	ditches	sketches	branches
squeaks	catches	punches	scratches	squeals	leashes

Answers will vary.

1a. _____

1b. _____

2a. _____

2b. _____

3a. _____

3b. _____

4a. _____

4b. _____

5a. _____

5b. _____

Exercise 8

Sentence Dictations Study these sentences and write them to dictation.

1. The encroaching waves and sheets of wind eroded the wide beaches, leaving patches where no grains of sand were left.

2. Their worst baseball game seats were back in the bleachers.

3. Still the wheel squeals and squeaks.

4. If an owner unleashes his dog in the forest and later catches him under a tree's branches, he could get scratches all over his body.

5. She picked off fleas and cockroaches with her tweezers.

Spellography • A Student Road Map to Better Spelling

Speed Read See how long it takes you to read these columns of words out loud from top to bottom. Record how you improve over three separate days, marking your times and errors.

tap	rob	hat	rod	road
tape	robe	heat	road	rode
				rowed
pan	rat	son	pant	reman
pane	rate	soon	paint	remain
not	tap	fed	bandit	belch
note	tape	feed	bandage	beach
				beech
bit	dim	cot	content	
bite	dime	coat	contain	wretch
				reach
hop	slop	stack	fair	
hope	slope	steak	fare	mad
				made
rip	pan	add	sees	maid
ripe	pain	aid	seas	
				upset
rid	got	clam	compel	upseat
ride	goat	claim	compete	
pal	set	red	repel	
pale	seat	read	rcpeat	

Day 1	Day 2	Day 3
Time:	Time:	Time:
_____	_____	_____
Errors:	Errors:	Errors:
_____	_____	_____

Finally: Take the Posttest, and record your score herc.   **Number Correct:** _____

Phonemic Awareness Activities

1. **Segmentation Activity** Hold up the number of fingers—or show the number of markers—that is equal to the number of sounds (phonemes) in each of these words.

sock	shock	shocked	bank	blank	blanks
/s/ /ŏ/ /k/	/sh/ /ŏ/ /k/	/sh/ /ŏ/ /k/ /t/	/b/ /ă/ /ng/ /k/	/b/ /l/ /ă/ /ng/ /k/	/b/ /l/ /ă/ /ng/ /k/ /s/

oak	soak	smoke	smoked	risk	brisk
/ō/ /k/	/s/ /ō/ /k/	/s/ /m/ /ō/ /k/	/s/ /m/ /ō/ /k/ /t/	/r/ /ĭ/ /s/ /k/	/b/ /r/ /ĭ/ /s/ /k/

tuck	stuck	struck	stroke	stroked	stoked
/t/ /ŭ/ /k/	/s/ /t/ /ŭ/ /k/	/s/ /t/ /r/ /ŭ/ /k/	/s/ /t/ /r/ /ō/ /k/	/s/ /t/ /r/ /ō/ /k/ /t/	/s/ /t/ /ō/ /k/ /t/

back	bake	break	broke	kick	click	clicked
/b/ /ă/ /k/	/b/ /ā/ /k/	/b/ /r/ /ā/ /k/	/b/ /r/ /ō/ /k/	/k/ /ĭ/ /k/	/k/ /l/ /ĭ/ /k/	/k/ /l/ /ĭ/ /k/ /t/

tank	thank	thanked	ache	fake	flake	flaked
/t/ /ă/ /ng/ /k/	/th/ /ă/ /ng/ /k/	/th/ /ă/ /ng/ /k/ /t/	/ā/ /k/	/f/ /ā/ /k/	/f/ /l/ /ā/ /k/	/f/ /l/ /ā/ /k/ /t/

tick	chick	trick	tricked	strict	streaked
/t/ /ĭ/ /k/	/ch/ /ĭ/ /k/	/t/ /r/ /ĭ/ /k/	/t/ /r/ /ĭ/ /k/ /t/	/s/ /t/ /r/ /ĭ/ /k/ /t/	/s/ /t/ /r/ /ē/ /k/ /t/

2. **Deletion Task** Say each word after deleting the identified sounds (phonemes).

speak without /s/	**click** without first /k/	**stuck** without /s/	**flake** without /f/
blank without /l/	**soak** without /k/	**click** without /l/	**struck** without /r/
break without /r/	**flake** without /l/	**smoke** without /m/	**brisk** without /s/

Phonemic Awareness Activities (Continued)

3. **Substitution Task** Substitute the first sound with the second sound to make a new word.

shock /sh/ – /l/	blank /b/ – /p/	soak /s/ – /p/	thank /th/ – /t/
speak /p/ – /l/	shock /sh/ – /s/	break /k/ – /d/	soak /k/ – /p/
reek /k/ – /p/	strike /ī/ – /ē/	flake /k/ – /m/	pack /ă/ – /ē/
shock /ŏ/ – /ā/	peck /ĕ/ – /ō/	Blake /l/ – /r/	speck /ĕ/ – /ī/

4. **Sound Reversals** Reverse the sounds (phonemes) to make a new word (**pit – tip**).

speak – keeps	make – came	Kate's – stake	Jake – cage
stock – cots	cope – poke	kin – Nick	cake – cake
puck – cup	stoke – coats	come – muck	keel – leak

LESSON 18
K is Special

Dictate words in the lesson word list for Pretest and Posttest administration. Modify the number of words as needed.

Lesson 18 Word List

1. shock	13. reckless
2. blank	14. flake
3. soak	15. reeking
4. smoke	16. briskly
5. thankful	17. stricken
6. stuck	18. blanket
7. strike	19. streaked
8. struck	20. earthquake
9. brake	21. meekly
10. leaking	22. thankless
11. package	23. courage
12. clicked	24. wreckage

Irregular words:

there, were, anything, young, women, before

Phoneme Manipulation (auditory) Create word magic by following these instructions.

Say **soak** without the /k/.

Say **smoke** without the /m/.

Say **struck** without the /r/.

Say **brake** without the /r/.

Change the /m/ in **stream** to /k/.

Change the /v/ in **favor** to /k/.

Change the /p/ in **stripe** to /k/.

Change the /k/ in **stricken** to /v/.

Change the /t/ in **smote** to /k/.

Change the first /s/ in **priceless** to /z/.

Spelling Concept: Review of /k/ sound spellings.

We will review the spellings of the /k/ sound in words with **closed** syllables (short vowel sounds), vowel + consonant + silent **-e** (**vc + -e**) syllables (long vowel sounds), and **vowel team** syllables.

1. The **-ck** spelling is used for /k/ after an accented short vowel:

la**ck**, he**ck**ler, ti**ck**et

2. If a vowel followed by a consonant is before /k/, then just use **-k**:

d**ark**, b**ank**, t**ask**

3. Spell /k/ with plain letter **k** if it comes after a long vowel sound or vowel teams:

r**ake**, l**ike**, s**oak**, p**eak**

Exercise 2

Fill in the first blank with the **-k** or **-ck** spelling. Then, in the second blank, give the number of the rule listed in the /k/ spelling concept review that you used for the spellings.

	Rule		Rule		Rule
plu _ck_	1	ba _ck/ke_	1/3	lo _ck_	1
spar _k_	2	bar _k_	2	stin _k_	2
lea _k_	3	bea _k_	3	smo _ck/ke_	1/3
li _ck/ke_	1/3	bu _ck_	1	mas _k_	2
lar _k_	2	bun _k_	2	lu _ck_	1
sa _ck/ke_	1/3	ra _ck/ke_	1/3	spe _ck_	1
see _k_	3	ree _k_	3	por _k_	2
bul _k_	2	ran _k_	2	dar _k_	2
pa_ck_ age	1	so _ck_ et	1	co _ck_ roach	1

Sort this lesson's study words among the four groups below based on the spelling pattern of the /k/ sound. Then, above each vowel letter in the groups, mark the sounded vowels as long (L), short, (S), <u>v + -r</u> (R), or schwa (ə). Mark any silent <u>-e</u> vowels as a diagonal line (/). Scoop under syllables to mark syllable divisions. (Do not include the irregular words.) You will not use all the words.

Lesson 18 Word List

1. shock	7. strike	13. reckless	19. streaked
2. blank	8. struck	14. flake	20. earthquake
3. soak	9. brake	15. reeking	21. meekly
4. smoke	10. leaking	16. briskly	22. thankless
5. thankful	11. package	17. stricken	23. (courage)
6. stuck	12. clicked	18. blanket	24. wreckage

Irregular words: there, were, anything, young, women, before

Short Vowel + -ck	**Vowel + Consonant + -k**	**Long Vowel + -k**	**vc + -e**
shock (S)	blank (S)	soak (L)	smoke (L /)
stuck (S)	thankful (S ə)	leaking (L L)	strike (L /)
struck (S)	briskly (S L)	reeking (L L)	brake (L /)
package (S ə /)	blanket (S ə)	streaked (L /)	flake (L /)
clicked (S /)	thankless (S ə)	meekly (L L)	earthquake (R L /)
reckless (S ə)			
stricken (S ə)			
wreckage (S ə /)			

Now, go back and underline <u>-ck</u>, consonant + <u>-k</u>, and <u>-k</u> spellings. Circle the word in the word list that starts with a /k/ sound spelled with the letter <u>c</u>.

Exercise 3b

Spelling Concept: Past tense, final **-ed** has three speech sounds: /t/, /d/, and /ed/.

Exercise 4a

What sound does **-ed** make in these spelling words?   /t/

> braked   clicked   streaked

Add -ed to the end of these spelling words.

Exercise 4b

shock _ed_   soak _ed_   blank _ed_   flake _d_

smoke _d_   reek _ed_   click _ed_

What sound does **-ed** make in these words?

The **-ed** ending in all of these words sounds like /t/; the voiceless

consonant sound /k/ is followed by the voiceless sound for **-ed**,

which is /t/.

Exercise 5

Suffix (Endings) Word Find Underline the suffixes (endings) in these words, which are among this lesson's study words. (Remember—a suffix is a meaningful part added to a root or a base word.) Select five of the suffix endings, write them as column headings, and list three other words with the same suffix.

thank**ful**	thank**less**	wreck**age**	brisk**ly**
reck**less**	leak**ing**	reek**ing**	click**ed**
meek**ly**	pack**age**	streak**ed**	

Example answers:

-ful	-ing	-ed	-less	-age
glassful	storming	checked	hopeless	storage
helpful	mending	intended	smokeless	postage
useful	inching	gripped	breathless	passage

Spelling Concept: Silent **-e** + suffix spelling rules.

1. If the suffix starts with a *vowel*, drop the silent **-e** before adding the suffix:

   > tak**e** + **ing** = taking
   >
   > bak**e** + **ed** = baked

2. If the suffix starts with a *consonant*, leave the silent **-e** alone:

   > lik**e** + **n**ess = **likeness**
   >
   > lik**e** + **l**y = **likely**

Exercise 6

Add the suffixes, as indicated, to these words. Then, tell which rule number you applied (**1** or **2**) to the spelling.

		Rule			Rule
smoke + less =	smokeless	2	brake + ed =	braked	1
joke + er =	joker	1	poke + ed =	poked	1
fake + er =	faker	1	meek + ly =	meekly	2
strike + ing =	striking	1	plate + ful =	plateful	2
rake + ing =	raking	1	broke + en =	broken	1
bike + er =	biker	1	snake + ing =	snaking	1

Exercise 7

Alphabet Soup Write each set of words in alphabetical order.

a b c d e f g h i j k l m n o p q r s t u v w x y z

Set 1:

meekly   reckless   courage shock   earthquake   thankless leaking   flake

1. courage

2. earthquake

3. flake

4. leaking

5. meekly

6. reckless

7. shock

8. thankless

Set 2:

strike   smoke stuck   shock   streaked soak   stricken

1. shock

2. smoke

3. soak

4. streaked

5. stricken

6. strike

7. stuck

Magic Squares Create at least 15 words from the letter combinations in this magic square.

Magic Square

e	FREE digraph	p
a	-k -ck	i
s	l	b

_____   _____

_____   _____

_____   _____

_____   _____

_____   _____

_____   _____

_____   _____

_____   _____

_____   _____

Spelling Concept: Adjectives and adverbs An **adverb** usually ends in **-ly** and tells more precisely how an action word (**verb**) is done. An **adjective** tells more about the **noun** it modifies.

Exercise 9

With your class or a partner, write each of these words into an expanded sentence. Then, indicate if you used the word as an adjective (**adj**) or an adverb (**adv**).

Answers will vary.

adj/adv

thankfully _____   _____

_____

thankless _____   _____

_____

meekly _____   _____

_____

stricken _____   _____

_____

briskly _____   _____

_____

reckless _____   _____

_____

reeking _____   _____

_____

Exercise
10

Sentence Dictations Write these sentences to dictation.

1. There's something leaking in the bottom of that package.

2. My blanket reeked of smoke after the basement fire.

3. In the wreckage of the earthquake, we were thankful for anything that was left unharmed.

4. After the briskly moving storm, I had the thankless job of cleaning sidewalks streaked with mud.

Speed Read Read this word list out loud from top to bottom on three different days. Record your reading times and errors each day.

lack	peck	bank	rocket
lake	speck	blank	sprocket
	speak	Blake	
bank			lick
bake	Jack	pock	flick
	Jake	poke	slick
lick		spook	
like	wick		luck
	week	stricken	puck
peck	weak	striking	pluck
peek	squeak		plucked
		picket	
clock	pick	ticket	
cloak	pickle	cricket	
	tickle		
trick		rank	
strike	peck	shrank	
	speck	shrunk	
mock	speak	shrink	
smock	squeak	shriek	
smoke			

Day 1	Day 2	Day 3
Time:	Time:	Time:
_____	_____	_____
Errors:	Errors:	Errors:
_____	_____	_____

Finally: Take the Posttest, and record your score here. **Number Correct:** _____

LESSON 19
To Urr is Human

Phonemic Awareness Activities

1. **Segmentation Activity** Hold up the number of fingers—or show the number of markers—that is equal to the number of sounds (phonemes) in each of these words.

urn	turn	return	returned
/er/ /n/	/t/ /er/ /n/	/r/ /ē/ /t/ /er/ /n/	/r/ /ē/ /t/ /er/ /n/ /d/

burp	bird	third	thirty	thirsty
/b/ /er/ /p/	/b/ /er/ /d/	/th/ /er/ /d/	/th/ /er/ /t/ /ē/	/th/ /er/ /s/ /t/ /ē/

limb	slim	swim	swimmer	irk	quirk	quirky
/l/ /ĭ/ /m/	/s/ /l/ /ĭ/ /m/	/s/ /w/ /ĭ/ /m/	/s/ /w/ /ĭ/ /m/ /er/	/er/ /k/	/k/ /w/ /er/ /k/	/k/ /w/ /er/ /k/ /ē/

berry	berries	raspberry	third	thirty	thirsty
/b/ /ār/ /ē/	/b/ /ār/ /ē/ /z/	/r/ /ă/ /z/ /b/ /ār/ /ē/	/th/ /er/ /d/	/th/ /er/ /t/ /ē/	/th/ /er/ /s/ /t/ /ē/

furry	fury	furious	air	fair	ferret
/f/ /er/ /ē/	/f/ /yūr/ /ē/	/f/ /yur/ /ē/ /ŭ/ /s/	/ār/	/f/ /ār/	/f/ /ār/ /ĭ/ /t/

surface	surplus	surprise	first	thirst
/s/ /er/ /f/ /ĭ/ /s/	/s/ /er/ /p/ /l/ /ŭ/ /s/	/s/ /er/ /p/ /r/ /ī/ /z/	/f/ /er/ /s/ /t/	/th/ /er/ /s/ /t/

Phonemic Awareness Activities (Continued)

2. **Vowel + -r (v + -r) Sound Match** The words given below contain each of the four **v + -r** sounds used in this week's words. Have students tell you the number of the **v + -r** sound they hear as you read the words.

1. /er/ (sir, her, fur)		2. /ir/ (ear, spirit)		3. /ār/ (air, ferry)		4. /yūr/ (fury)	
miracle	2 /ir/	stern	1 /er/	merit	3 /ār/	thirst	1 /er/
mural	4 /yūr/	squirm	1 /er/	cherry	3 /ār/	cheery	2 /ir/
occur	1 /er/	sheriff	3 /ār/	irrigate	2 /ir/	berry	3 /ār/
surprise	1 /er/	sure	1 /er/	ferret	3 /ār/	mirage	1 /er/
heritage	3 /ār/	irritate	2 /ir/	nocturnal	1 /er/	curious	4 /yūr/

3. **Deletion Task** Say each word after deleting the identified sounds (phonemes).

colder without /k/	**turn** without /t/	**thunder** without /th/
stern without /s/	**label** without first /l/	**flurry** without /l/
thirsty without /ē/	**jerky** without /k/	**thirsty** without /s/
gurgle without second /g/	**swirl** without /s/	**wilder** without /l/

4. **Sound Reversals** Rearrange the position of the letters or letter sounds around the **v + -r** sounds to make new words (**carp – park**, **lark – Carl**).

verse – serve	**perch – chirp**	**dearth – third**

Dictate words in the lesson word list for Pretest and Posttest administration. Modify the number of words as needed.

Lesson 19 Word List

1.	burger	13.	swimmer
2.	squirm	14.	skirmish
3.	Saturday	15.	berry
4.	very	16.	bury
5.	merit	17.	ferret
6.	spirit	18.	grungier
7.	thinner	19.	luxury
8.	thirsty	20.	sheriff
9.	Mercury	21.	disturbed
10.	cherry	22.	irrigate
11.	thirty	23.	irritate
12.	surprise	24.	irregular

Irregular words:

special, Christmas, caught, than/then, twos

Spelling Concept: The sounds /er/ (accented) and /ər/ (unaccented) are usually spelled with three vowel + **-r** (**v + -r**) spelling patterns: **er**, **ir**, and **ur**. These spelling patterns sometimes stand for other sounds as well. The spelling pattern **er** represents a "short **e**" plus /r/ sound in some words, and **ir** represents a "long **e**" plus /r/ sound in some words. These sound-spelling relationships are less common, but each has its place in the **er**, **ir**, and **ur** family of words.

Sound Matching Listen while your teacher talks you through this exercise.

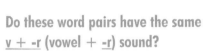

Do these word pairs have the same **v + -r** (vowel + **-r**) sound?

very – merry	Y	surprise – perfect	Y
nurture – purge	Y	Carey – Harold	Y
skirmish – absurd	Y	fearful – miracle	Y
spirit – spiral	N	terror – furry	N
cherry – error	Y	burly – bury	N
irritate – urgent	N	marry – merry	N

Underline the **v + -r** combinations in this lesson's spelling words. (Do not include the irregular words.) Then, sort the words based on the **v + -r** syllable spellings and corresponding sounds. Star (★) the words whose syllable spellings and sounds apply to more than one column.

Lesson 19 Word List

1. b<u>ur</u>g<u>er</u>
2. squ<u>ir</u>m
3. Sat<u>ur</u>day
4. v<u>er</u>y
5. m<u>er</u>it
6. sp<u>ir</u>it
7. thinn<u>er</u>
8. thi<u>r</u>sty
9. M<u>er</u>c<u>ur</u>y
10. ch<u>err</u>y
11. thi<u>r</u>ty
12. s<u>ur</u>prise
13. swimm<u>er</u>
14. sk<u>ir</u>mish
15. b<u>err</u>y
16. b<u>ur</u>y
17. f<u>err</u>et
18. grungi<u>er</u>
19. lux<u>ur</u>y
20. sh<u>er</u>iff
21. dist<u>ur</u>bed
22. <u>irr</u>igate
23. <u>irr</u>itate
24. <u>irr</u>egul<u>ar</u>

Irregular words: special, Christmas, caught, than/then, twos

er
(rhymes with **her**)

Mercury ★

swimmer

burger ★

thinner

grungier

ir
(rhymes with **sir**)

squirm

thirty

thirsty

skirmish

ur
(rhymes with **fury**)

Mercury ★

er
(rhymes with **ferry**)

very

cherry

ferret

merit

berry

sheriff

ir
(rhymes with **spear**)

spirit

irritate

irrigate

irregular ★

ur
(rhymes with **fur**)

burger ★

surprise

disturbed

Saturday

luxury

ur
(rhymes with merry)

bury

ar
(rhymes with better)

irregular ★

Spelling Concept: There is a common sound that the letters <u>er</u>, <u>ir</u>, and <u>ur</u> can repre-sent, but each spelling can also stand for other sounds.

Exercise 3

Fill in the blanks below with <u>er</u>, <u>ir</u>, or <u>ur</u>. Then, give the number of the <u>v + -r</u> sound you hear.

1. /er/ (as in **fur, her, sir**)	2. /ir/ (as in **ear, spear**)	3. /ār/ (as in **air, ferry**)	4. /yūr/ (as in **fury**)

	Number			Number
squ <u>ir</u> m	1		v<u>er</u>y	3
sp <u>ir</u> it	2		s<u>ur</u>e	1
Sat <u>ur</u> day	1		th <u>ir</u> ty	1
ch<u>er</u>ry	3		sk <u>ir</u> mish	1
m<u>er</u>it	3		b<u>er</u>ry	3
m<u>ur</u>al	4		t<u>er</u>rible	3
st<u>er</u>n	1		f <u>ir</u> st	1
sh<u>er</u>iff	3		dist<u>ur</u>b	1
m <u>ir</u> ror	2		f<u>er</u>ret	3
Th<u>ur</u>sday	1		t<u>er</u>m	1
lux <u>ur</u> y	1		b<u>ur</u>y	3
M<u>er</u>c<u>ur</u>y	1,4		swimm<u>er</u>	1

Exercise 4

Ringo Bingo Fill in any six squares on the Ringo Board with a pronunciation symbol and an example key word containing **one** of the four **v + -r** sounds that we are studying this week (refer to the numbered boxes in Exercise #3). Add one free square anywhere on the board. Write the answer words from Exercise #3 on game cards. Mix the cards and place them facedown, making a pick pile (you may add other words from this lesson to the pick pile if you want). Put a marker on a blank square that matches the **v + -r** sound in the word you pick from the card pile. Five word-sound matches in a column, a row, or diagonal wins.

Example board:

Ringo Board

/er/	/ir/	/yūr/	/ār/	/yūr/
/ir/	/ār/	/er/	/yūr/	/ār/
/yūr/	/ār/	free	/ir/	/er/
/yūr/	/er/	/ir/	/er/	/ār/
/ār/	/ir/	/er/	/yūr/	/ir/

Divide this lesson's words into syllables by scooping under them. Remember to divide between consonants in a <u>vccv</u> pattern, to divide after a long vowel in an open (<u>vcv</u>) syllable, and to keep <u>v + -r</u> sequences together.

burger	merit	Mercury
swimmer	ferret	disturbed
squirm	spirit	cherry
skirmish	grungier	irrigate*
Saturday	thinner	thirty
berry	luxury	irritate*
very	thirsty	surprise
bury	sheriff	irregular*

*Note: These are advanced words from Latin roots. Watch out for the schwa (ə)! Look up these words in a dictionary.

Spelling Concept: Why it's the Y Rule! This is the thrilling and defining moment when you, dear student, get to learn the mysteries of the **Y Rules for endings**. Why not?

1. When a word ends in **y**, preceded by a consonant, the **y** always changes to **i** when you add a suffix:
   s**py** + **ed** = s**pied**   noi**sy** + **ly** = noi**sily**

2. **BUT** if the suffix starts with an **i** (as in **-ing**), then keep the **y**. You can't have two **i**'s in a row in an English word (unless the word derives from Scandinavia, like **skiing**):
   s**py** + **ing** = s**pying**   de**fy** + **ing** = de**fying**

3. If the **y** is part of a vowel team (**ey**, **uy**, **ay**, **oy**), the **y** never changes:
   pr**ay** + **ed** = pr**ayed**   b**uy** + **er** = b**uyer**

Exercise 6

Add the endings to these words. Then, give the number of the **Y Rule** you followed to spell the word correctly.

	Rule		Rule
murky + ness = _murkiness_	1	luxury + ous = _luxurious_	1
obey + ed = _obeyed_	3	hurry + ing = _hurrying_	2
grungy + er = _grungier_	1	curry + ed = _curried_	1
turkey + s = _turkeys_	3	curry + ing = _currying_	2
curly + est = _curliest_	1	dirty + ing = _dirtying_	2
valley + s = _valleys_	3	ferry + ing = _ferrying_	2
fury + ous = _furious_	1	ferry + ed = _ferried_	1
cheery + ness = _cheeriness_	1	pay + ment = _payment_	3
stay + ed = _stayed_	3	berry + (e)s = _berries_	1
bury + ing = _burying_	2	cherry + (e)s = _cherries_	1
bury + ed = _buried_	1	sturdy + er = _sturdier_	1

Exercise 7

Word Detective Referring to this lesson's word list, answer each of these questions. (Do not include the irregular words.)

Lesson 19 Word List

1. burger	9. Mercury	17. ferret
2. squirm	10. cherry	18. grungier
3. Saturday	11. thirty	19. luxury
4. very	12. surprise	20. sheriff
5. merit	13. swimmer	21. disturbed
6. spirit	14. skirmish	22. irrigate
7. thinner	15. berry	23. irritate
8. thirsty	16. bury	24. irregular

Irregular words: special, Christmas, caught, than/then, twos

a. What word is the name of a planet? _Mercury_

Which god is this planet named for? _This planet is named for the Roman_
god Mercury. Mercury is the messenger and god of commerce and
travel, as well as the god of cunning and theft. Mercury is the planet
nearest to the sun.

b. What planet and god is Saturday named for? _Saturday is named for the_
planet and god Saturn. Saturn is the Roman god of agriculture, as
well as the father of Jupiter.

c. Which words are homophones? _berry_   (_bury_)

Circle the one that means "to put into the ground." Give four examples of the other one.
Example answers:
raspberry   _blueberry_   _strawberry_   _blackberry_

d. Which three words use the same prefix?

irregular   irritate   irrigate

The prefix **ir-** was changed from **in-** to match the root; **in-** / **ir-** can have different meanings. As a prefix, **in-** / **ir-** can mean "into or toward" (as in **insert**), or it can mean "not" (as in **inexact**). Underline the word(s) in which the changed prefix **ir-** means "not," and box the word(s) in which the changed prefix **ir-** means "into or toward." Then, list three more words that use this prefix and underline or box them accordingly, too.

_____   _____   _____

Example answers:

(these **ir-** prefixes mean "not," so the words should be underlined): irrational, irrelevant, irreplaceable, irresponsible, irrevocable

(these **ir-** prefixes mean "into or toward," so the words should be boxed): irradiate, irrupt

e. Write the word formed from the Anglo-Saxon root **furct**, meaning "little thief." ferret

Use the word in sentences that show its noun and verb meanings. Label the noun (n) and verb (v) uses.

Example answers:

(n) The ferret liked to play hide-and-seek with Dillon.

(v) We need to ferret out all criminals from their hiding places.

f. The **-er** suffix can be used to show comparison (as in **faster**), or to indicate someone who does something (as in **hiker**).

Which study words use the suffix **-er** to show comparison? thinner   grungier

Which study word uses **-er** to indicate "a person who does something"? swimmer

Which study word is a form of the word hamburger? burger

In the word **hamburger**, the **-er** ending lets us know a hamburger comes from Hamburg. Where is Hamburg, and what does it have to do with hamburgers?

Hamburg is a city in Germany; it's where hamburgers were invented.

g. Which study word defines a small-scale battle? skirmish

Can you find words in a dictionary that mean a major, large-scale battle?

Example answers:

onslaught, clash, brawl, assault, barrage

Spelling and Parts of Speech: Adjectives.

Adjectives are used to describe someone or something (a noun). Adjectives can be modified with the comparative (**-er**) and the superlative (**-est**) endings to show the degree of quality (for example: the **thinner** horse, the **thinnest** horse). **Thinner** and **thinnest** are adjectives that tell something about the noun **horse**.

The word **very** also means "to a high degree." Sometimes, we can add an **-er** or **-est** ending to indicate degree; sometimes, we can use the word **very**.

Use the adjectives large, grungy, thirsty, and irregular to describe nouns of your choice.

Example answers:

Adjective	Noun	Adjective	Noun
The large	whale	The grungy	hobo
The thirsty	horse	The irregular	heartbeat

Now, change the phrases in Exercise #8a to show comparison or degree by using the word endings **-er** or **-est**, or the word **very**.

Example answers:

Adjective	Noun	Adjective	Noun
The largest	whale	The grungiest	hobo
The very thirsty	horse	The very irregular	heartbeat

Spelling and Parts of Speech: Nouns can be names of things or ideas that are abstract; that is, they can't be touched, seen, or felt.

Exercise 9

Separate the nouns in this lesson's word list by type among the four categories. (Do not include the irregular words.) Star (★) any words that could apply to more than one category.

Lesson 19 Word List

1. burger	7. thinner	13. swimmer	19. luxury
2. squirm	8. thirsty	14. skirmish	20. sheriff
3. Saturday	9. Mercury	15. berry	21. disturbed
4. very	10. cherry	16. bury	22. irrigate
5. merit	11. thirty	17. ferret	23. irritate
6. spirit	12. surprise	18. grungier	24. irregular

Irregular words: special, Christmas, caught, than/then, twos

Person	Place	Thing	Abstract Idea
swimmer	Mercury	burger	spirit ★
sheriff		ferret	surprise ★
		skirmish	luxury ★
		Saturday	merit ★
		cherry	
		berry	
		spirit ★	
		surprise ★	
		luxury ★	
		merit ★	

Spelling and Parts of Speech: Verbs tell something that you do or did (an action performed).

Exercise 10

List some of the verbs in this lesson's word list. (Do not include the irregular words.) Then, tell where, why, what, when, how, or to whom that action is or was done.

Lesson 19 Word List

1. burger	9. Mercury	17. ferret
2. squirm	10. cherry	18. grungier
3. Saturday	11. thirty	19. luxury
4. very	12. surprise	20. sheriff
5. merit	13. swimmer	21. disturbed
6. spirit	14. skirmish	22. irrigate
7. thinner	15. berry	23. irritate
8. thirsty	16. bury	24. irregular

Irregular words: special, Christmas, caught, than/then, twos

Verb	where, why, what, when, how, to whom

Example answers:

I _squirm_ quietly in class when I'm spelling v + -r words.

I _surprise_ myself each morning, because I still look funny.

I _bury_ my dog's bone at night by the bushes because it's fun.

I _disturbed_ the neighbors with my harmonica-playing in the back yard.

I _irrigate_ my family's fields to produce vegetables for city folk.

I _irritate_ my dad every day by hanging wet clothes on his hat.

Exercise 11

Alphabet Soup Circle eight of the words in this lesson's word list and write them in alphabetical order. (Do not include the irregular words.)

Lesson 19 Word List

1. burger	9. Mercury	17. ferret
2. squirm	10. cherry	18. grungier
3. Saturday	11. thirty	19. luxury
4. very	12. surprise	20. sheriff
5. merit	13. swimmer	21. disturbed
6. spirit	14. skirmish	22. irrigate
7. thinner	15. berry	23. irritate
8. thirsty	16. bury	24. irregular

Irregular words: special, Christmas, caught, than/then, twos

a b c d e f g h i j k l m n o p q r s t u v w x y z

1. _____ 2. _____ 3. _____

4. _____ 5. _____ 6. _____

7. _____ 8. _____

All study words in alphabetical order:

1. berry	9. irrigate	17. spirit
2. burger	10. irritate	18. squirm
3. bury	11. luxury	19. surprise
4. cherry	12. Mercury	20. swimmer
5. disturbed	13. merit	21. thinner
6. ferret	14. Saturday	22. thirsty
7. grungier	15. sheriff	23. thirty
8. irregular	16. skirmish	24. very

Sentence Dictations Study these phrases, idioms, and figures of speech, and then write them. Then select eight of them, and use them in sentences. Recite your sentences to the class.

flipping burgers

squirm like a worm

very merry Christmas

caught in the act

_____

_____

_____

_____

merit raise

school spirit

to err is human

special treatment

_____

_____

_____

_____

thirsty as a sponge

thirty-something

cherry red

luxury liner

_____

_____

_____

_____

larger than life

bury the hatchet

terrible twos

red as a rose

_____

_____

_____

_____

1. _____

_____

2. _____

_____

3. _____

_____

4. _____

_____

5. _____

_____

6. _____

_____

7. _____

_____

8. _____

_____

Speed Read Read these lists of contrasting words out loud from top to bottom, as fast as you can. Record the time it takes you to read them—**with no errors**—on three consecutive days.

squirt	irritate	air	merit
squirm	irrigate	fair	merry
squirming	irrigated	ferret	meritorious
	irritated		
curt		regular	thin
skirt	third	irregular	thinner
skirted	thirty	irregularly	thinnest
	thirsty	regulation	
slim			burly
swim	surface	disturb	burlier
swimmer	surplus	disturbing	burliest
	surprise	undisturbed	
furry			
fury	bury	cherry	
furious	berry	cheery	
	raspberry	churning	
	strawberry		
grungy		purse	
grungier	surprise	disperse	
grungiest	surmise	disburse	
	surround	disbursement	

Day 1	**Day 2**	**Day 3**
Time:	Time:	Time:
_____	_____	_____
Errors:	Errors:	Errors:
_____	_____	_____

Finally: Take the Posttest, and record your score here. **Number Correct:** _____

Phonemic Awareness Activities

1. **Segmentation Activity** Hold up the number of fingers—or show the number of markers—that is equal to the number of sounds (phonemes) in each of these words.

for	fort	forty	were	worst	world
/f/ /or/	/f/ /or/ /t/	/f/ /or/ /t/ /ē/	/w/ /er/	/w/ /er/ /s/ /t/	/w/ /er/ /l/ /d/

air	tear	stare	stared	car	scar	scarred
/ār/	/t/ /ār/	/s/ /t/ /ār/	/s/ /t/ /ār/ /d/	/k/ /ar/	/s/ /k/ /ar/	/s/ /k/ /ar/ /d/

ore	core	score	scorch	were	worry	worthy
/or/	/k/ /or/	/s/ /k/ /or/	/s/ /k/ /or/ /ch/	/w/ /er/	/w/ /er/ /ē/	/w/ /er/ /th/ /ē/

ate	rate	trait	traitor	is	it	visit	visitor
/ā/ /t/	/r/ /ā/ /t/	/t/ /r/ /ā/ /t/	/t/ /r/ /ā/ /t/ /er/	/ĭ/ /z/	/ĭ/ /t/	/v/ /ĭ/ /z/ /ĭ/ /t/	/v/ /ĭ/ /z/ /ĭ/ /t/ /er/

2. **Vowel + -r (v + -r) Sound Match** The words given below contain each of the four v + -r sounds used in this week's words. Have students tell you the number of the v + -r sound they hear as you read the words.

1. /er/ (her, worm)	2. /or/ (corn, sport)	3. /ār/ (air, care)	4. /ar/ (tar)
forty 2 /or/	world 1 /er/	starch 4 /ar/	stare 3 /ār/
visitor 1 /er/	starry 4 /ar/	scorch 2 /or/	worst 1 /er/
tarnish 4 /ar/	declare 3 /ār/	worry 1 /er/	compare 3 /ār/
forgery 2 /or/, 1 /er/	spectator 1 /er/		
farthest 4 /ar/	scared 3 /ār/		
scarred 4 /ar/	director 1 /er/, 1 /er/		
torment 2 /or/	February 3 /ār/		

Phonemic Awareness Activities (Continued)

3. **Deletion Task** Say each word after deleting the identified sounds (phonemes).

forty without /ē/	**world** without /d/	**stare** without /s/	**starry** without /ē/
scorch without /ch/	**worthy** without /<u>th</u>/	**worry** without /ē/	**scared** without /s/
scar without /s/	**stork** without /k/	**glory** without /l/	**spark** without /s/
flavor without /l/	**labor** without /b/	**short** without /t/	**normal** without /n/+/m/
forth without /th/	**flair** without /l/	**scorned** without /n/	**charming** without /ch/

4. **Sound Reversals** Rearrange the position of the letters or letter sounds around the <u>v + -r</u> sounds to make new words **(germ – merge, lark – Carl)**.

art – tar	**stork – courts**	**march – charm**	**dark – card**
tarps – parts	**starch – charts**	**arts – star**	**carp – park**
north – thorn	**scar – arcs**	**cork – cork**	**Marla – alarm**

LESSON 20
Car Horn

Dictate words in the lesson word list for Pretest and Posttest administration. Modify the number of words as needed.

Lesson 20 Word List

1. forty
2. world
3. starch
4. stare
5. visitor
6. starry
7. scorch
8. worst
9. tarnish
10. declare
11. worry
12. traitor
13. worthy
14. compare
15. spectator
16. forgery
17. farthest
18. inspector
19. scared
20. scarred
21. tormentor
22. Delaware
23. director
24. February

This week, we are once again studying how the consonant sound /r/ (**ruffle**) hypnotizes vowels with its charming ways to produce those peculiar vowel plus **-r** (**v + -r**) sounds. What is *really* strange is that Thunker's dog Bess makes most of these **v + -r** sounds herself (especially when she sees a cat!). Maybe these **v + -r** lessons will help you to better communicate with dogs and annoy cats. Who knows?

Spelling Concept: The sounds /ar/ (as in **far**) and /or/ (as in **corn**) are usually spelled with **ar** and **or**. However, these **v + -r** combinations also spell other sounds. The letter combination **ar** represents a "long **a**" plus /r/ sound (as in **fare**) in some words, and the letter combination **or** represents an /er/ sound (as in **odor**) in some words, especially when after **w** (as in **worm**). These sound-spelling relationships are less common, but each has its place in the large **ar** and **or** family of words.

Exercise 1

Sound Matching Listen while your teacher talks you through this exercise.

Do these word pairs have the same (s) or different (d) **v + -r** sound?

Say the **v + -r** sound that is in each word of the pair.

stark – stork (d)	search – scorch (d)
compare – repair (s)	word – heard (s)
tarnish – garnish (s)	air – bear (s)
scary – starry (d)	far – there (d)
director – inventor (s)	
worry – wormy (s)	
starred – stared (d)	
splurge – worst (s)	

Underline the **v + -r** spelling combinations in this lesson's spelling words. Then, sort the words based on the **v + -r** syllable spellings and corresponding sounds. Star (★) the words whose syllable spellings and sounds apply to more than one column.

Lesson 20 Word List

1. f<u>or</u>ty
2. w<u>or</u>ld
3. st<u>ar</u>ch
4. st<u>ar</u>e
5. visit<u>or</u>
6. st<u>ar</u>ry
7. sc<u>or</u>ch
8. w<u>or</u>st
9. t<u>ar</u>nish
10. decl<u>ar</u>e
11. w<u>or</u>ry
12. trait<u>or</u>

13. w<u>or</u>thy
14. comp<u>ar</u>e
15. spectat<u>or</u>
16. f<u>or</u>gery
17. f<u>ar</u>thest
18. inspect<u>or</u>
19. sc<u>ar</u>ed
20. sc<u>ar</u>red
21. torment<u>or</u>
22. Delaw<u>ar</u>e
23. d<u>ir</u>ect<u>or</u>
24. Febru<u>ar</u>y

or (as in **sport**)	**or** as final syllable (as in **doctor**)	**wor** (as in **word**)
forty	visitor	world
forgery ★	traitor	worry
scorch	spectator	worst
tormentor ★	inspector	worthy
format ★ ★	tormentor ★	work ★ ★
porch ★ ★	director ★	worm ★ ★
	dictator ★ ★	
	indicator ★ ★	

ar (as in **car**)	**ar** (as in **care**)	**er** (as in **her**)
starch	stare	forgery ★
tarnish	compare	fertile ★ ★
scarred	February	perch ★ ★
starry	declare	**ir** (as in **stir**)
farthest	Delaware	
bark ★ ★	scared	director ★
target ★ ★	flare ★ ★	dirt ★ ★
	marry ★ ★	firm ★ ★

Now, **find** two more words that apply to each group.

(Words with two stars [★★] are examples of additional words.)

Exercise 2b

Spelling Concept: We can use the **v + -r** sound to help us decide correct spellings.

Exercise 3

Fill in the blanks below with the letters **or** or **ar**. Then, give the number of the **v + -r** sound you hear.

1. /er/ (as in **worm**, **doctor**)	2. /or/ (as in **corn**)	3. /ār/ (as in **dare**, **care**)	4. /ar/ (as in **tar**, **car**)

	Number		**Number**
f_or_ty	2	w_or_st	1
st_ar_ch	4	st_ar/or_e	3/2
st_ar_ry	4	trait_or_	1
decl_ar_e	3	sc_or_ch	2
f_ar_thest	4	inspect_or_	1
sc_ar_ed	3	comp_ar_e	3
_or_gan	2	Delaw_ar_e	3
sc_ar_red	4	t_or_ment	2
b_or_der	2	ch_ar_ge	4
direct_or_	1	w_or_ry	1
Febru_ar_y	3	w_or_ld	1
t_ar_nish	4	f_or_gery	2

Exercise 4

Ringo Bingo Fill in any six squares on the Ringo Board with a pronunciation symbol and an example key word containing **one** of the four <u>**v + -r**</u> sounds that we are studying this week (refer to the numbered boxes in Exercise #3). Add one free square anywhere on the board. Write the answer words from Exercise #3 on game cards. Mix the cards and place them face-down, making a pick pile (you may add other words from this lesson to the pick pile if you want). Put a marker on a blank square that matches the <u>**v + -r**</u> sound in the word you pick from the card pile. Five word-sound matches in a column, a row, or diagonal wins.

Example board:

Ringo Board

/er/	/ar/	/ār/	/or/	/er/
/ar/	/ār/	/or/	/er/	/ar/
/ār/	/or/	free	/er/	/ar/
/or/	/ār/	/er/	/or/	/ār/
/ar/	/er/	/or/	/ār/	/ar/

Divide this lesson's words into syllables by scooping under them. Remember to divide between consonants in a <u>vccv</u> pattern, to divide after a long vowel in an open (**vcv**) syllable, and to keep <u>v + -r</u> sequences together. Pronounce each word by syllable and see if a classmate can blend the word together.

forty	declare*	scared
visitor*	compare	director*
tarnish	inspector	stare
worthy	Delaware*	worst
farthest	starch	traitor
tormentor	scorch	forgery
world	worry	scarred
starry	spectator	February*

*****Note:** These words are quite tricky. Look them up in a dictionary and watch out for schwa!

Magic Squares Form words using the letters in each of these magic squares. Create at least 10–15 words from the letters in each square.

Magic Square

t	s	f
h	or	e
b	m	n

_____ _____

_____ _____

_____ _____

_____ _____

_____ _____

_____ _____

_____ _____

Magic Square

b	k	d
c	ar	e
f	t	s

_____ _____

_____ _____

_____ _____

_____ _____

_____ _____

_____ _____

Spelling and Grammar: The spelling and form of a word often denotes its part of speech. For example, the **-or** ending often indicates a noun, in the form of a person who does something; and a **-y** ending often indicates an adjective, a word that describes a noun. Other descriptive words have **-ary**, **-ery**, and **-ory** endings.

Exercise 7

Adjectives are used to describe something or someone. You can describe a swamp as a "murky, infested swamp." The words **murky** and **infested** are adjectives that tell us something about the swamp. In the first blank, write an adjective from this lesson's spelling words. Write the thing that you are describing in the second blank.

Lesson 20 Word List

1. forty
2. world
3. starch
4. stare
5. visitor
6. starry
7. scorch
8. worst
9. tarnish
10. declare
11. worry
12. traitor
13. worthy
14. compare
15. spectator
16. forgery
17. farthest
18. inspector
19. scared
20. scarred
21. tormentor
22. Delaware
23. director
24. February

Example answers:

Adjective	Noun
The _starry_	_night_
The _worthy_	_cause_
The _worst_	_chicken_
The _farthest_	_journey_

Spellography • A Student Road Map to Better Spelling

Nouns are persons, places, ideas, or things. Write the nouns from this lesson's word list where they belong in the columns below. Star (★) the words that can be used as either a noun or a verb.

Person	Placc	Thing	Idea
visitor	world	stare ★	worry ★
traitor	Delaware	forgery	
spectator		February	
inspector		starch ★	
tormentor		tarnish ★	
director			

Verbs are words for actions or states of being. After selecting four verbs from this lesson's word list, write them in the "Verb" column. Then, finish the sentence by telling more about where, why, what, when, how, or to whom that action is or was done.

Example answers:

Verb	Where, Why, What, When, How, or to Whom

I _scorched_ _the turkey in the old oven because the_

thermometer broke.

I _starch_ _my shirts so that they look crisp and clean_.

I _declared_ _my intentions so that they knew I wanted_

the job.

I _compare_ _prices when shopping to get the best deals_.

Lesson 20 Word List

1. forty	7. scorch	13. worthy	19. scared
2. world	8. worst	14. compare	20. scarred
3. starch	9. tarnish	15. spectator	21. tormentor
4. stare	10. declare	16. forgery	22. Delaware
5. visitor	11. worry	17. farthest	23. director
6. starry	12. traitor	18. inspector	24. February

Spelling Concept: Many words from the Latin layer of the English language are built from roots, prefixes, and suffixes. The words **spectator** and **inspector** come from the root **spect**, which means "to look at, to see."

Make or find as many words as you can that use the root **spect**. Try using these prefixes in forming your words: <u>in-</u>, <u>re-</u>, <u>a-</u>, <u>ex-</u>, <u>per-</u>, <u>pro-</u>, <u>retro-</u>, and <u>sus-</u>. Also, add different suffixes.

"spect" Words

Example answers:

inspect	inspected
respect	respectable
aspect	aspects
expect	cxpected
perspective	prospecting
prospect	suspects
retrospect	
suspect	

Exercise 11

After the letter w, the letters or sound like /er/ (as in **worm**). List at least five words from your spelling list and a dictionary that use the **w + or** spelling. Then, find at least five words that use the letters **ar** after **w** (as in **war**).

What sound does the **ar** make after **w**? _____/or/_____

w + or Words

world

worst

worry

worthy

worse ★

word ★

w + ar Words

ward ★

warm ★

warp ★

warden ★

warn ★

wart ★

Starred words are example answers.

Exercise 12

Word Detective Refer to this lesson's word list to complete these statements or answer these questions.

a. The month after January is _____ February. _____ .

b. Six words for people who do specific things are _____ visitor _____ ,

_____ traitor _____ , _____ spectator _____ , _____ inspector _____ ,

_____ tormentor _____ , and _____ director. _____ .

c. Find four words that can be used as both nouns and verbs.

_____ starch _____ , _____ stare _____ , _____ worry _____

_____ tarnish _____ .

d. What is a crime that you can be arrested and jailed for?

_____ forgery _____

e. The name of one of America's smallest states is

_____ Delaware _____ .

Alphabet Soup Write each set of words in alphabetical order.

a b c d e f g h i j k l m n o p q r s t u v w x y z

Set 1:

farthest Delaware forty declare February director forgery

1. declare

2. Delaware

3. director

4. farthest

5. February

6. forgery

7. forty

Set 2:

scorch stare spectator scared starry scarred starch

1. scared

2. scarred

3. scorch

4. spectator

5. starch

6. stare

7. starry

Spellography • A Student Road Map to Better Spelling

Exercise 14

Sentence Dictations Make up a question that uses both words in each of these word pairs. The class will use the best questions for dictation.

Example answers:

1. **worst, traitor** Who was the worst traitor in American history?

2. **compare, forgery** Can you compare the two paintings and tell which is the forgery?

3. visitor, spectator Is the visitor a spectator or a performer?

4. farthest, world Where in the world is the farthest place from your home?

5. worthy, director Did you find a worthy director for your play?

6. scarred, scorch When you scorch your arm, does the skin get scarred?

7. starry, world Is there a starry world out there with life as we know it on Earth?

8. inspector, declare Did the inspector declare the building safe?

Professor Thunker thought that he could get rich by writing a soap opera set in the early days of the Paleo Era, which occurred about 12,000 years ago. Thankfully, this project went the way of the Paleo people—although this prehysteric draft was mysteriously found inside a woolly mammoth horn, half-buried near the entrance to the Shelburne Museum. Time yourself reading this passage on three different days. Record your time and errors.

The Lives of the First Thunkers

Way back before computers or nose-hair clippers—at the birth of history—there lived a muscular brute named Urrg and his charming partner, Cora. Together they shared a sparse cave overlooking a sandbar by the Champlain Sea. Each morning, Urrg and Cora would carefully sharpen barbs on their harpoons before going forth to the sea to spar with the fierce beasts therein. Returning with swordfish, shark, or marlin, they would sear the fish in strips over sparking flames. Beside the dark waters, under sparks and stars, Urrg and Cora would pass a birch bark bowl—steaming with morsels of charred fish—back and forth. Later, keeping warm under thick furs, Urrg and Cora would stare past the flames and sparks to the stars and worship the spirits that brought them together and kept them from harm.

Day 1	Day 2	Day 3
Time:	Time:	Time:
—————	—————	—————
Errors:	Errors:	Errors:
—————	—————	—————

Challenge Activity
Underline all of the **v + -r** combinations in this reading. How many did you find? _67_

Finally: Take the Posttest, and record your score here. **Number Correct:** _____